1001 Sidesplitting One-Liners & Some Wisdoms

1001 Sidesplitting One-Liners & Some Wisdoms

James Dines

Published by
BCM, Inc

Published by BCM, Inc,
PO Box 636, Belvedere, California, 94920.

10 9 8 7 6 5 4 3 2

ISBN 0-9649689-1-6
Library of Congress Card Number 2001091363

Cover design by Jan Camp, Berkeley, California

Printed in the United States of America by Data
Reproductions

DEDICATION

This book is dedicated to my parents in gratitude for their unconditional love, encouragement to enjoy entertaining people and striving to be the best I could be.

Table of Contents

PREFACE

A smile is free, and laughter is extremely important because it is the foundation of a healthy mentality. It is crucial to include humor in writing and public speaking because when I have included them audiences have been most encouraging. In fact, they themselves requested that I put together a collection such as this! Even a subject as generally humorless as financial reporting could not only be enlivened to make it more enjoyable, but it gets points across better and is remembered more easily. Besides, it's enormously enjoyable to please an audience!

In my years of having been the editor of *The Dines Letter* I came across many little gems, also what I call "wisdoms" by some of the great thinkers of the past, and I thought it might be useful to writers, public speakers, or those who simply would like to enjoy a good belly laugh. I have never seen a joke book, combined with great sayings from the past, quite like this unique one.

To spice things up there is some off-color content, just so that you are aware before you go any further. The sections on "Women's Lib" might be construed as anti-male, "Politically Incorrect" as anti-female, the sections on marriage and dating as anti-both of them, but I am personally in favor of all of them. There is no "ethnic humor" herein. I didn't mean to offend anyone, and all is intended to be in the spirit of good fun; this book is just my encapsulated hope that it would cheer you up!

We've tried to give credit to those who first uttered the enclosed, but if we misquoted anybody, gave the wrong credit, or credit needs to be given, please let us know and we would be glad to add them to future editions.

Speaking of which, if you know of any spectacular sidesplitting one-liners or wisdoms, please let us know. If we include them in future editions, we will acknowledge your contribution by adding your name and a thanks.

While this book has been arranged alphabetically by topics, and you could select a topic from the Table of Contents which follows, it has also been written so that you could read it straight through (if your ribs could take the splitting)!

If you'd like to give copies of this book as a gift, for a holiday perhaps, in order to spread the fun and laughter you enjoyed, then see the coupon at the end.

Finally, I would like to give special credit to my staff, who helped enormously in putting this book together, chuckling all the way. That includes: Heather Hale, Pavan Johal, Alvin Lew, Peter Mason, Dennis Palabyab and Tania Toporkov. Plus the cover design by Jan Camp is unique. May you live every day of your life!

James Dines

1001 Sidesplitting One-Liners & Some Wisdoms

Accidents

Some guy hit my fender and I said to him, "Be fruitful and multiply," but not in those words.

Woody Allen

I have a theory that airlines deliberately want you to wear seat belts . . . so as to save the part of the torso with the wallet!

When there's an oil spill, they put a rope around it. Imagine, a rope around it, when they couldn't even contain it with a ship around it!

Advice

All a bachelor has to do to discover his hidden faults is to get married!

Good cowboy advice is always to drink upstream from the herd!

When birds of a feather flock together, you'd better stay out from underneath them!

If you really want to be a person of letters, change your name to "occupant"!

A good scare is worth more than good advice!

If you want people to notice your faults, start giving advice!

Advise those seeking stock-market advice to make their own decisions . . . and that then they'll always be right!

If you want the world to beat a path to your door, build your house on a jogging path!

If you don't have a leg to stand on, it's best not to kick!

Trust in Allah, but tie your camel.
Arabian proverb

Never give advice in a crowd.
Arabian proverb

When you come to a fork in the road, take it!
Yogi Berra's advice for making tough decisions

A curved line in the loveliest distance between two points.   *Mae West*

You will always find a few Eskimos ready to tell the Congolese how to cope with the heat.
Stanislaw J Lec

Never try to save money on food, shoes or good advice. *Lillian Dines*

Alzheimer's

I'm a psychic, but I have Alzheimer's . . . So I know what I'm going to forget!

If you forget where your car keys are, that's just forgetfulness. But if you forget what your car keys are for, that's Alzheimer's!

What if you get déjà vu and amnesia at the same time?

Don't be like the married man looking forward to Alzheimer's, so that he could be with a different woman every night. Only to discover the bad news that his mother-in-law has a twin sister!

It might be the truth that an elephant never forgets, but, then, again, what's an elephant got to remember?

A doctor informed his patient, after an examination, that he had some "bad news" and then "even-worse news." The patient asked for the bad news first, and the doctor told his patient that he had cancer. Horrified, the patient braced himself and, asked for the "even-worse news," whereupon the doctor told the patient that he had Alzheimer's. At which time the patient seemed greatly relieved and exclaimed: "Well, at least I don't have cancer!"

There's one thing about Alzheimer's . . . every day you wake up you make new friends.

Rodney Dangerfield

Anger

Did you get up on the wrong side of the web today?

Necessity is the mother of tension.

Never get your shorts in a bunch!

It takes *you* to make a quarrel.

Try to remember that for every minute you're angry, you lose sixty seconds of happiness.

When angry count to four; when very angry, swear.
Mark Twain

His huff arrived and he departed with it.
Alexander Woollcott

Powerless rage can work miracles.
Stanislaw J Lec

If you are patient in one moment of anger, you will escape a hundred days of sorrow. *Chinese proverb*

Make no promises when seized by joy; write no letters when seized by anger. *Chinese proverb*

Arrogance & Humility

"Yes men" have nodding in common!

If you wish at last to see perfection on this planet, read job applications!

It's what we learn after we know it all that really counts!

We didn't all come over on the same ship, but we're all in the same boat!

At least an egomaniac doesn't go around talking about other people.

Morality is living so as to avoid guilt, blame, shame, and regrets later.

You've no idea what a poor opinion I have of myself – and how little I deserve it.   *W S Gilbert*

Every man values himself more than all the rest of men, but he always values others' opinion of himself more than his own.   *Marcus Aurelius*

Monkeys are superior to men in this: when a monkey looks into a mirror, he sees a monkey.
    Malcolm de Chazal

And where does she find them?
    Dorothy Parker
(on hearing that Claire Boothe Luce was kind to her "social inferiors")

Never underestimate a man who overestimates himself.   *Franklin D Roosevelt*
(about General Douglas MacArthur)

Bald

Don't worry about losing your hair, think of it as gaining face!

Grass doesn't grow on a busy street . . . but it doesn't grow on concrete either!

Hair today, gone tomorrow.

A hair on the head is worth two on the brush!

Maybe the economy's biggest problem is not production, but distribution . . . which strikes a bald-headed man with peculiar force every time he shaves!

One thing about baldness: it's neat.   *Don Herold*

Birth

People are giving birth underwater now. They say it's less traumatic for the baby because it's in water. But certainly more traumatic for the people in the pool.   *Elayne Boosler*

I can remember so far back in my past that I can recall being a fast little ... sperm. I remember the day of the big race – there were millions of us. I was at her cervix ... I was seaman, first class!   *Jim Carrey*

Blondes

What's the best way to drown a blonde? Put a mirror at the bottom of the pool!

Why do blondes pencil in their eyebrows? They have to draw the line somewhere!

Did you hear how the blonde kept from getting raped? She beat off her attacker!

What do you call a brunette walking down the street with one blonde on each side of her? . . . "Interpreter"!

The highway policeman pulls over a car, and asks to see the blonde's license. He sees she's not too bright and begins to pull his zipper down. She cries out, "Oh no, not another breathalyzer test!"

Blondes also prefer gentlemen!

The blonde excitedly told her girl friend that she was so grateful for the three-dozen roses her boyfriend had just sent her that she was looking forward to spending the weekend with her legs in the air. The girl friend asked, "Can't you afford a vase?

Many a dumb blonde is a smart brunette!

Boring

If you want to walk the streets safely at night, carry a projector and slides from your last vacation!

The secret of being a bore is to tell everything!

Excuse me, my leg has gone to sleep. Do you mind if I join it?

A bore is someone who is here today and here tomorrow.

Poke someone's forehead a few times, and when they ask what you are doing reply, "Looking for the fast-forward."

He has occasional flashes of speech that make his long silences perfectly delightful.

Anybody who could watch boring Fedhead Greenspan for several straight days runs the risk of being declared legally brain dead. Greenspan needs to drop bread crumbs for himself at the beginning of his paragraphs to remember where he is going. In one of his speeches he complained that he had been talking for half an hour but that there was so much noise he could hardly hear himself talk, when someone from the back shouted out, "That's all right, you're not missing anything!"

I'm not saying that he makes long-winded speeches, but at the end of one of his long stories he said, "Well, to make a long story short . . .," when somebody in the back shouted, "Too late!"

It seems that boredom is one of the great discoveries of our time. If so, there's no question but that you must be considered a pioneer.

Some people brandish statistics to make their point, as if they were a threat of boredom.

It is only shallow people who do not judge by appearances.   *Oscar Wilde*

A professor is someone who talks in someone else's sleep.   *W H Auden*

My grandfather had a special rocking chair built that would lean forward rather than backward, so that he could fake interest in any conversation.
Steven Wright

The only way a woman can ever reform a man is by boring him so completely that he loses all possible interest in life. *Oscar Wilde*

Never take sides in anything. Taking sides is the beginning of sincerity, and earnestness follows shortly afterwards, and the human being becomes a bore. *Oscar Wilde*

Brain Twisters

A professor of Greek history took his torn suit to a tailor in Greece. The tailor looked at the ripped pants and said, "You rippa deese?" "Yes," replied the professor, "Eumenides?"

I woke up this morning feeling like a teenager. Unfortunately, I couldn't find one, so I decided to come to work!

Necessity is the martyr of invention.

The word "the" can be important. For example, there's a big difference between saying "my wife gave me crabs," or that she gave me *"the* crabs." The first is your crab dinner and the second is *you're* the crab's dinner!

The sure cure for feeling listless is to write a list!

The mediocre are always at their best!

I was daydreaming about my inability to fantasize!

Sometimes, chaste makes waste!

I recently picked up a book on levitation . . . and couldn't put it down!

All wounds heal and all heels wound!

What's the capital of Ohio? . . . It's the big letter at the beginning!

It's futile to try to throw away a garbage can . . . the Sanitation Engineers keep returning it!

It takes the crack of a dawn to break a beautiful day . . . before night falls.

How many times can you subtract the number 5 from 25? . . . Only once. Thereafter, it's subtracted from 20, and so on!

Change is a good thing, particularly if you're planning on taking a bus!

The exterminators came today and now I have a terrible headache . . . all that stomping!

Next time, don't drive as if you own the road – drive as if you own the car!

When someone wants you to follow their train of thought, make sure they don't have a loco motive!

Why did the scientist install a knocker on his door? To win the Nobel Prize!

If a dairy diary is moomoirs, what is a bull behind a tapestry? . . . When you can't see the taurus for the frieze!

A man walks into a doctor's office with a duck attached to his head, and the doctor asks, "What can I do for you?" and the duck says, "I want you to remove this wart on my foot!"

If your parents had no children, the odds are high you won't either!

All generalizations are wrong, except this one.

What do you do when the only person who can make you stop crying is the person who made you cry?

I'd give my right arm to be ambidextrous.
                                                    Yogi Berra

You can observe a lot by just watching. *Yogi Berra*

It's not too far. It just seems like it is.   *Yogi Berra*

We were overwhelming underdogs.   *Yogi Berra*

Last night I baited a mousetrap with a picture of cheese . . . I caught a picture of a mouse!
                                                    Henny Youngman

I have a large collection of seashells . . . on the beaches all over the world. Maybe you've seen it?
                                                    Steven Wright

I have a microwave fireplace, so I can have a whole evening of fire in eight minutes!   *Steven Wright*

The guy who lives across the street from me has a circular driveway, and he can't get out.

Steven Wright

If I can melt dry ice, can I swim without getting wet?   *Steven Wright*

I bought some powdered water and now I don't know what to add!   *Steven Wright*

I woke up one day and everything in my home had been stolen and replaced with exact replicas!

Steven Wright

I like to reminisce with people I don't know, which is why I try to skate on the other side of the ice!

Steven Wright

I went to a museum where they had all the heads and arms from the statues that are in all the other museums.   *Steven Wright*

I've been getting into astronomy, so I installed a skylight. The people above me are furious!

Steven Wright

The farther he went West, the more convinced he was that the wise men came from the East.
Sydney Smith

Birds of a feather flock together because, how could birds flock any other way?   *Henny Youngman*

Breaking Wind

Things are really good when you can finally fart through silk!

He who drives an ass must of necessity smell its fart.   *West African proverb*

Beans, beans, the magical fruit, the more you eat the more you toot!

That went over like a fart in a submarine!

Business

A beautiful and sexy woman walked up to a man in a bar and said, "I'll do anything you want for $200." He replied, "Terrific. Come paint my house!"

If at first you don't succeed . . . it's probably not your father's business.

A man boasted to his friend that he was doing extremely well in business. Asked how, he explained that he bought gizmos for twenty cents each and sold them for nineteen cents each. The friend asked how he could possibly make money doing that, and was boldly informed that, "I make it up in volume!"

Financial television is now so desperately hungry for material that it is scraping the top of the barrel. Which lets us be entertained by people we wouldn't have in our homes!

Why is the flag at the Post Office at half mast? . . . They're hiring!

Whenever I hear about foreigners buying America out, I wonder whether Native Americans say, "At least they're paying for it!"

The worst part about conventions is that they prove how expendable you are at the office!

Many companies have nothing to do with football, but they will nonetheless wind up in the hands of a receiver!

Remember, "work ethic" isn't what it used to be
... acquired!

Someone complaining about business conditions said, "Just look at this suit I'm wearing: the wool was grown in Australia, the cloth was woven in England, the thread comes from India, the suit was made in Baltimore and I bought it in Manhattan.""So what's the problem?" "Isn't it wonderful that so many people can make a living out of something I can't pay for!"

Even window installers take great panes to please their customers!

The secret of why some last so long in business is that it's never too late to have a happy childhood.

What did one successful farmer say to the other? "Let's get together for a *plower* lunch really soon!"

The function of a depression is to return property to its rightful owners. And who are those rightful owners? Those who wind up with the property!

The world is divided into victims and predators, and you have to defend yourself against both!

Profit is the corporate report card.

"Now you can borrow all you need to get out of debt." *(Sign seen posted in a bank.)*

To be a leader of men one must turn one's back on men.

Any new venture goes through the following stages: enthusiasm, complication, disillusionment, search for the guilty, punishment of the innocent, and decoration of those who did nothing!

Never decide to buy something while listening to a salesman.   *Edmund C Berkley*

The salesman knows nothing of what he is selling save that he is charging a great deal too much for it.
                                                    Oscar Wilde

A man trying to sell a blind horse always praises its feet.   *German proverb*

Go the extra mile. It's never crowded.
                                 Executive Speedwriter Newsletter

No nation was ever ruined by trade.
                                                    Benjamin Franklin

Cannibals

One cannibal turned to his dinner partner and said, "I'm having a ball!" The other said, "Well then, you're eating too fast!"

When one cannibal told another that he couldn't stand his mother-in-law, the cannibal advised that he should just push her aside and enjoy the rest of his soup!

The latest movie on cannibalism is doing very well. In fact, they're coming out with a sequel: "The Second Helping."

Children

If you want to teach your kids to count, give them different allowances!

Teach your children the value of money . . . borrow from them!

Do you know the difference between broccoli and boogers? . . . Kids won't eat broccoli!

Isn't it wonderful that the summer is over and your kids are finally going back to someone who can handle them?

Children should be seen and not had!

The way to get along with kids is to treat them like tiny adults . . . who are stupid!

It's better to have loved and lost, than to have to do homework for the kids every night!

The best way to get your kid to shovel the snow is to say that it's okay to use the car!

The easiest way to get your children to call you is to send them a check . . . and forget to sign it!

Wouldn't it be great if all children behaved the way you think you did when you were a kid?

Sound travels very slowly: the things you tell them when they're children reach them when they're about 40!

There's nothing wrong with children that reasoning won't aggravate!

Heredity is what people believe in until their child begins to behave like a delinquent!

Teacher: "Here's a question for you: If there are three crows on a fence and you shoot one, how many are left?"
Student: "None. The shots scared them off."
Teacher: "Wrong, but I like the way you think."
Student: "Okay, now let me ask you a question: If three women are eating ice cream, and one sucks it, the other licks it, and the third chews it, which one is married?"
Teacher: "The one who sucks it."
Student: "Wrong. The one with the ring, but I like the way you think!"

Father: "Don't play with yourself, or you'll go blind."
Boy: "Can't I just do it until I need glasses?"
Father: "If you masturbate, you'll go blind."
Son: "Dad. Dad! . . . I'm way over here!"

The secret of dealing successfully with a child is not to be its parent!

The advantage of having a large family is that at least one of the children might not turn out like the others.

Children are a great comfort to you in your old age
. . . and they help you reach it sooner!

If you don't want your children to hear what you're saying, pretend you're talking to them!

A five-year-old little girl saw a stallion mounting a mare in a field and asked her mother what they were doing. The embarrassed mother replied that the one on top had hurt his front hoof and the one on the bottom was helping him get back to the barn. The tiny child shook her head and said sadly, "That's just the way real life is with people also . . . you try to help somebody and you get screwed!"

Many families in America who did not send their children to camp for the summer went over to their neighborhood schools, patted the front door, saying, "Soon!"

I spent the last three days child-proofing my apartment . . . but they still seem to be able to get in!

By the time a child realizes that maybe his parent was right, he usually has a child who thinks he's wrong!

Kids are the screwing you get for the screwing you got!

If God intended for me to reason with my children, he wouldn't have made them smaller than me!

One should avoid swimming in pools with any children nearby . . . if only to avoid the warm spots!

You might say that having children is a *fetal* mistake!

If God had wanted sex to be fun, He wouldn't have included children as punishment!

Learning to dislike children at an early age saves a lot of expense and aggravation later in life!

Children despise their parents until the age of 40, when they suddenly become just like them, thus preserving the system!

You see, the trouble with these days as compared to the 1980's is that teenage nerds no longer rebel and leave home!

A child is a parent's lance into eternity.

Virtue is what parents told us to do because they didn't . . . so we don't!

Dad: "Son, I never kissed a girl until I met your mother. Will you be able to say the same thing to your son?"
Son: "Yes, dad, but not with such a straight face!"

The peacock is beautiful, but it takes a stork to deliver the goods!

What is more enchanting than the voices of young people, when you can't hear what they say?
Logan Pearsall Smith

I'm beginning to understand those animals you read about where the mother has got to hide the young so the father won't eat them.   *W C Fields*

A guest on Groucho's "You Bet Your Life" television show was a woman who had given birth to 22 children. "I love my husband," the woman explained sheepishly. "I love my cigar too" Groucho said, "but I take it out once in a while."

Children are like the homeless, shuffling around the house and pestering you: "Could I have a dollar? Got any food around here? I'm hungry. I'm missing a shoe. Can I have a ride?"   *Kathleen Madigan*

I'm scared of sex, because you could get something terminal . . . like a kid! So the only way to avoid that is to abstain . . . from drinking! My mom is 60, and she's only had sex with one man . . . but she can't remember his name!   *Wendy Liebman*

If you're a child at twenty, you're a jackass at twenty-one.   *Shlomo Zipkin*

Familiarity breeds contempt . . . and children.
                              Mark Twain

A happy childhood is poor preparation for human contacts.   *Colette*

Somewhere on this globe, every ten seconds, there is a woman giving birth to a child . . . She must be found and stopped.   *Sam Levenson*

It is no wonder that people are so horrible when they start life as children.   *Kingsley Amis*

The owl always believes his son is a hawk.
Hungarian proverb

I take my children everywhere . . . but they always find their way back home. *Robert Orben*

Reprimand your child regularly every day. You might not know why, but the kid does.
Harry Hershfield

The reason grandparents and grandchildren get along so well is that they have a common enemy.
Sam Levenson

The best way to give advice to your children is to find out what they want, and then advise them to do it.
Harry S Truman

The first half of our life is ruined by our parents and the second half by our children. *Clarence Darrow*

When I was little, my grandfather used to make me stand in the closet for five minutes without moving. He said it was elevator practice. *Steven Wright*

Class

He lacks "class," by which I mean what a butcher would have were he a surgeon.

Cultivation of the uncultured results in a culture.

The girls I used to date said they were seeking a man who was kind, sensitive and rich . . . so I said, "Look, if I had those qualities, would I be with you?"
Rodney Dangerfield

He who sells to the masses will live with the classes, while he who sells to the classes will live with the masses!

Never speak disrespectfully of society, Algernon. Only people who can't get in to it do that. *Oscar Wilde*

Never wrestle with a pig. You get dirty and, besides, the pig likes it.　　　　*Cyrus Ching*

My grandmother is over eighty and still doesn't need glasses . . . she drinks right out of the bottle.
Henny Youngman

Clinton

Bill Clinton earned one-million dollars last year. He paid $100,000 in taxes . . . and that doesn't even count what he got under the table!

When Clinton invites a woman to his office, it's usually not a standing invitation!

President Clinton once granted a White House franchise to Hooters, presumably with the willing retail attitude of first-come-first-served. Then, the cover-up!

Clinton's latest legal defense was, "I was sucked into it!"

They've just taken a survey of women as to whether they'd have an affair with President Clinton, and 63% said, "Never again"!

As an example of the amazing obsession with Clinton's ins and outs, despite the Lewinsky scandal, Clinton's poll – you should forgive the expression – readings keep rising. And the White House is now saying that "they were only kissing." Or, as Clinton would say, "I never impaled!"

It's crucial to have a sense of history in trying to understand the Internet. It's like President Clinton feeling great kinship with Sir Thomas Moore, who got his head chopped off by the king in 1535. Why? Because Clinton also feels persecuted, vilified and, since he lost Monica, headless!

Now that Clinton has left office, he is back to making the hard choices!

They've just announced that they're adding two new faces to Mt. Rushmore: Bill Clinton's!

Someday, Clinton's tombstone will read, "Here, yet again, lies William Jefferson Clinton"!

President Clinton was eager to leave a legacy as a great president, having compared himself to some of the giants of the past . . . but he'll probably only go down in history as the president who came after Bush!

Clinton was thrown out of Heaven and on the way down, he passed the pope, who was gliding skyward. The pope said, "At last, I'm going to meet the Virgin Mary." Clinton mumbled, "Not since the last 20 minutes!", as he headed lower.

Why did the Clintons have only one child? Some unkind people allege that Hillary had a vasectomy!

If lust is when the lion lies down with the limb, I figure Clinton is happy with the Internet because it begins with "intern." Ostensibly, there was one job he wanted more than being president!

Zippergate prompted Hillary to introduce her book called, "It Takes an Entire Village to Keep an Eye on My Husband's Zipper"!

Wasn't all the attention to our president's crotch overblown?

President Clinton wears woolen underwear . . . presumably to keep his ankles warm!

President Clinton went to Africa, and was treated like such a hero that they're now calling him, "The Great White-Trash Hunter."

That Hillary Clinton puts up with it all proves marriage is nature's way of keeping people from fighting with strangers!

Which movie does Bill Clinton show to seduce White House interns? *Free Willy*!

How did Clinton keep Monica Lewinsky away from the White House? . . . He offered to send Ted Kennedy over to give her a ride!

Bill Clinton deals with Hillary on the theory that it's easier to get forgiveness than permission. Hillary deals with Bill on the theory that no husband has been shot while doing the dishes!

As Clinton once said to an intern, supporting the notion that the devil finds work for idle glands . . . "There's no place to go but down!"

When asked his opinion of his chances of prosecuting the president, Ken Starr said, "It's an open and slut case!"

Hillary found out she was pregnant. She was so infuriated that she went straight to the nearest phone and called the Oval Office. When Bill answered, Hillary said, "You rotten jerk, you got me pregnant!" There was silence on the other end of the line, which infuriated her even further. "You got me pregnant!" she accused indignantly. No answer. "Answer me you loser," she shrieked, "You got me pregnant"!
Bill finally replied, "Uh . . . who is this?"

A rogue is charming if kept carefully harmless!

Did you hear that Bill Clinton is supporting a new math curriculum in our nation's schools? . . . He wants everyone to know that 50 can go into 21 without getting 5 to 10!

If the White House were a ship, and cash the wind, he could have been blown anywhere!

Clinton's a real survivor, he lied and then two House speakers resigned. But, typical of Clinton, he's still standing and everybody else is going down!

Clinton's been bragging that when he was president employment was up, the economy was up, but, most important, now his zipper is up!

President Clinton was *very* unpopular, yet he was re-elected in 1996 because he was in touch with the people . . . some more than others.

Bill Clinton's definition of safe sex; when Hillary's out of town!

Does anybody here know what Ted Kennedy has that Clinton desperately wanted? A dead girlfriend!

What's the worst thing Bill Clinton ever heard during sex? "Honey, I'm home!"

Coming out against mutual funds might be as gauche as using the word "liposuction" around Bill Clinton. Indeed, the European press called Clinton, "President Bush." Except for Spain . . . which called him "El BJ"!

White House employees are no longer allowed to use the polite expression "Pardon me!"

Asked by a reporter, "You've been sued several times for the same crime, aren't you the least bit ashamed?" President Clinton replied, "No, I don't believe a man should be ashamed of his convictions."

The ever-impressionable Monica said that when she first looked into the eyes of President Clinton, she saw something unexpected – his belt buckle!

We can be grateful that, at least we were spared the news that President Clinton tried to hang mistletoe under his desk!

What do Hillary and Monica have in common? They both blow a little dope!

Clinton is like a bigamist, the kind of man who loves not wisely, but two well!

There were many VIPs at a huge funeral, including Cardinal John O'Connor, the Clintons, the Gores, the Bushes. But President Clinton was near tears . . . not for the deceased, but it had been a long time since he had seen Hillary on her knees! *Bill Maher*

Thousands of women have been lured into Clinton's bed with only these three words . . . "Hillary's not here." *Jay Leno*

I think President Clinton misunderstood the role of the president, which is to screw the country as a whole, not individually. *Betsy Salkind*

We have already thought of a rallying cry for the next election: The Clintons are coming – hide the women and silver!" *David Horowitz*

Clinton went to visit India where he is extremely popular . . . perhaps it's because over there Monica Lewinsky is considered sacred! *Bill Maher*

Comparing

It's like learning that a suicidal twin killed his brother by mistake!

That would be as likely as a turkey voting for an early Thanksgiving!

That would be as likely as Bette Midler getting Tom Cruise on the rebound!

If you walk around like a hammer, everything looks like a nail!

There's not much of the charm of the forest left in a can of mushroom soup!

Style is as necessary to life as lubrication is to sex!

That's like saying marriage is the sole cause of divorce!

That might send markets down further than Jesse Jackson's face on Father's Day!

Married men have better halves, while bachelors have better quarters!

Buying Internet stocks for profit has gotten like asking why men get married . . . so they don't have to hold in their stomachs anymore!

That would be like asking Jesse Jackson to run Planned Parenthood!

It's said that cannibals used to eat many missionaries, perhaps proving that one man's meat is another man's parson!

That's as unlikely as people who raise rabbits enjoying raisins!

There could be a coming stock-market decline, it dropping faster than a mink running away from an aging movie star!

One might wonder why it is that when you transport something by car it is called a "shipment," and when you send it by ship it's called "cargo"!

The easiest way for gardeners to tell the difference between young plants and weeds is to pull up everything; if they come back again, they're weeds!

A cat can have kittens in the oven, but that doesn't make them biscuits!

I need that like a moose needs a hat rack!

That would be like blaming wet sidewalks for having caused rain. Or cancer for having caused tobacco!

They were as colorful as a glass of distilled water!

It was so hot . . . how hot was it? It was so hot that fire hydrants were looking for dogs!

That would be like having Dr Kevorkian teach the Heimlich maneuver!

We find that as unlikely as going to a gas station these days where they speak English. And where it's also "full serve"!

It's like being married to a nymphomaniac . . . it's great for the first three weeks!

That would be like a reindeer's opinion of Chernobyl!

That would be like defining the word "toad" as what happens to an illegally parked frog!

That's like saying a grave digger is the last person in the world to let you down.

That would be as likely as Dr Kevorkian taking a check from a client!

Asking Americans to select a favorite between any two politicians is like asking which is your favorite Menendez brother!

That's as mean as sending a get-well card to a hypochondriac!

Asking which is the better presidential candidate is like calling Moe "the smart Stooge"!

When you lose money in a casino, it's like the stork getting blamed for what is usually the fault of a lark!

That's like putting Dracula in charge of the blood bank!

It's like childhood, that happy period when nightmares occur only during sleep!

That would be like hiring Freddie Kruger as your baby sitter!

That's as scarce as a grocery cart with all four wheels going in the same direction!

That would be like putting slinkies on an escalator!

That would be like getting circumcised on a roller coaster!

Crime

In America, we'll try everything once, except criminals. And speaking of criminals, Congress is the legislative body that makes the laws and whose chaplain prays for the country!

His life started from a single cell and, if justice is done, a lot of it will end there!

Straight trees have crooked roots.

Crime has gotten so bad these days that corporate accounting departments are starting to include muggings on their balance sheets!

A day in prison is a day dead.

Society often forgives the criminal, but never forgives the dreamer!

Of all the arguments against capital punishment, there's no answer to the riposte that at least that criminal won't do it again!

You think that the gas chamber is "cruel and unusual punishment"? How about finishing off murderers the way *they* killed their victims . . . such as going on a picnic with Jeffrey Dahmer?

Perhaps the biggest crime committed by transvestites would be male fraud!

Imagine the tabloid headline, "Mob Bumps Off Einstein Because He Knew Too Much"!

What do prisoners use to call each other?
Cell phones!

Carjackings are so bad that we're now prepared to recommend that you drive with the club *on*!

Criminals don't get caught because they're "stupid," but because of the secret desire of all gamblers to lose.

If life is to be valued and secured, it must be known that anyone who takes the life of another forfeits his own.   *Ernest Van den Haag*

The truest jests sound worst in guilty ears.
John Ray

A man walked up to me and said, "Do you see a cop around here?" I said, "No." He said, "Stick 'em up!"
Henny Youngman

Cocaine is God's way of saying you're making too much money. *Robin Williams*

Critics

A critic is a man created to praise greater men than himself, but he is unfortunately never able to find one!

Asking an artist for his opinion of a critic is like asking a lamp post what it thinks of dogs and pigeons!

A reviewer of a ballet wrote: "The trouble is, all the seats faced the stage!"

If the shoe doesn't fit, it isn't your shoe!

There has never been a statue in honor of a critic.
Jean Sibelius

Drama critics are there to show gay actors what it's like to have a wife.   *Hugh Leonard*

Don't pay any attention to critics . . . don't even ignore them.   *Sam Goldwyn*

Currencies

The minister of a church in the financial district ended his sermon with, "Remember that there will be no buying and selling of currencies in Heaven!" One parishioner leaned over to another and said, "It doesn't matter, because that's not where currencies are going!"

I've seen the new currency, the euro, and it says on it, "In Gutenberg we trust"!

With the US dollar lower, it no longer talks common cents!

Someday dollars to doughnuts will be an even bet!

A currency crisis means that there was a time when parents taught their kids the value of a dollar; today, they try to keep the bad news from them as long as possible!

Years ago it was children who didn't know the value of their currency, and now it's nations.

These days, paper currencies worldwide are like a bunch of staggering drunks holding each other up.

Why is a deteriorating currency bullish? Because it's exhilarating to spend an inheritance.

Dating

The way it is is the way it is. You can't make something that it is not. You can't make a silk purse out of a sow's ear . . . but a smart girl knows how to get a fur coat out of an old goat!

One man's folly is often another man's wife!

Abstinence makes the heart go wander.

Absolute truth is for children . . . and people who don't want sex!

No pleasure endures unseasoned by variety!

What's the difference between Woody Allen and the New York Rangers? Woody Allen scores before the first period!

All a man really wants is a pretty face . . . provided it changes often enough!

A good line is the shortest distance between two dates!

The lonely widow struck up a conversation with a man by asking him what he did for a living, and he responded by saying he had been in jail for twenty years. She asked him what for, and he said that it was for having killed his third wife, that he had shot her. The widow asked what had happened to his second wife, and he said that he had poisoned her. She asked about his first wife and he admitted to having pushed her out of a window. The lonely widow reflected on all this for a moment, and asked, "So may I assume that you're single now?"

Going to single's bars is like trying to catch a trout by going fishing in a bathtub!

What makes men chase women they have no intention of marrying? The same urge that makes dogs chase cars they have no intention of driving!

After complaining that his mother disliked every girl he brought home, a friend advised the boy to bring home a girl that looked just like his mother. Some time later, he met his friend again and said he had followed his advice, brought someone home who looked exactly like his mother, with the same personality, and was practically her twin. The friend asked what happened and was curtly informed that, "My father couldn't stand her!"

They did a survey and found out that the best pick-up line in a bar was, "Hi, I'm John." The least successful line was, "Pull my finger!"

It's easy for a woman to get rid of a man . . . simply give him what he demands; it's rarely what he truly wants, so he'll leave!

The High State of Truth is like a light going on, and can be compared with a woman finally having figured out what a sperm and a man in a single's bar have in common . . . They both have a one-in-a-million chance of becoming a human being!

I've been living with somebody for a long time, but I recently moved out. Now my mother misses me!

When she asked him whether they could just be friends, he said, "Okay, let's go out and find some broads!"

A survey asked if I wanted to marry or stay single. They asked if I wanted to go out with many idiots or stay home with the same idiot. They asked if I wanted to go to bars and talk about stuff in which I was not interested, or stay home and hear again what I had heard before. They asked if I wanted to be alone, with a dirty magazine touching myself . . . or did I want to be single!

(Jerk holding out two clenched fists toward a woman in a bar) "Guess what I've got in my hand and I'll sleep with you." . . . "An elephant?" "Okay, close enough!"

Big news from the zoo – they finally got the pandas to mate. All it took was for the male panda to get a Porsche!

Many a woman who got tired of trying to get a pearl out of an oyster has settled for getting a diamond out of an old crab!

In the language of flowers, the yellow rose means friendship, the red rose means love and the orchid means business!

When Rita Rudner was asked for her secret for perfect relationships, she replied: "Let the other person be themselves . . . and make believe they're someone else!"

I had a date last night. She took off all her clothes, looked at me and said . . . "Get away from that window!" . . . She had a tattoo above her left breast . . . it was difficult staying excited while Yosemite Sam was giving me the finger. She said she had to shave her legs, shave under her armpits and then, take a shower . . . Hey, I just need to jump into my Batman suit and I'm ready!   *Mark Roberts*

I only like two kinds of men; domestic and imported!   *Mae West*

It's not the men in my life that counts – it's the life in my men!   *Mae West*

I've always had a weakness for foreign affairs.
                                                        Mae West

I generally avoid temptation unless I can't resist it.
                                                        Mae West

Give a man a free hand and he'll try to put it all over you.   *Mae West*

A youth with his first cigar makes himself sick – a youth with his first girl makes other people sick.

Mary Wilson Little

Here's to woman! Would that we could fall into her arms without falling into her arms.

Oscar Wilde

A French woman, when double-crossed, will kill her rival; the Italian woman would rather kill her deceitful lover; the English woman simply breaks off relations – but they will all console themselves with another man!

Charles Boyer

What is a date really, but a job interview that lasts all night?

Jerry Seinfeld

A woman should never chase a man . . . unless of course he's getting away.

Zsa Zsa Gabor

Happiness is a good cigar and a good woman – it depends on how much happiness you can handle.

George Burns

There's no such thing as romance in our day. Women have become too brilliant; nothing spoils a romance so much as a sense of humor in a woman.

Oscar Wilde, 1893

Organ donations are a big thing these days. Thousands are waiting for an organ . . . Hopefully, including my date tonight.   *Bill Maher*

Never try to impress a woman, because if you do she'll expect you to keep up to that standard for the rest of your life.   *W C Fields*

Every man I meet wants to protect me. I can't figure out from what.   *Mae West*

She's descended from a long line her mother listened to.   *Gypsy Rose Lee*

He who has one woman has all women; he who has all women has no woman.   *Spanish proverb*

Beauty has a short-lived reign.   *Socrates*

A woman will flirt with anybody in the world, as long as other people are looking on.   *Oscar Wilde*

Women prefer being amused without being loved, rather than being loved without being amused.
          Mme Derieux

God created the flirt as soon as He made the fool.
Victor Hugo

Woman begins by resisting a man's advances and ends by blocking his retreat. *Oscar Wilde*

To err is human, but it feels divine! *Mae West*

When I'm good, I'm very, very good. But when I'm bad . . . I'm better. *Mae West*

He who hesitates is a damned fool. *Mae West*

There are terrible temptations which it requires strength and courage to yield to. *Oscar Wilde*

It's not true I had nothing on. I had the radio on. *Marilyn Monroe (after being asked if she slept nude)*

Women – they're just as afraid of us as we are of them. Uh, no, I meant *snakes*! *Norm MacDonald*

Women's styles might change, but their designs remain the same. *Oscar Wilde*

High heels were invented by a woman who had been kissed on the forehead. *Christopher Morley*

What do I want most in life? . . . A chick swinging from the chandelier with a pickle in her mouth.

Andrew Dice Clay

Death

Give us levity or give us death!

Punishment during an average person's lifetime consists of 20 years of parents asking where you're going, 40 years of having a spouse asking the same question and, in the end, mourners wondering also!

A man was weeping at a cemetery, wailing loudly, moaning, "Why did you die? How could you have died?"
A nearby mourner asked him whether the person who died was a relative.
The weeping mourner said, "No," and then again wailed "Why did you die?" The nearby mourner asked, "If it's someone you never met, why are you crying so loud? Who's buried here?" And the weeping man said, "My wife's first husband!"

This guy dies and leaves the shortest will. It said "Being of sound mind, I spent all my money!"

Henny Youngman

When she passed away she was cremated. At least we *think* that's what did it!

Death is the debt we pay to nature.

There's no fun in a graveyard, so give me my flowers now!

The difference between the presidency and Elvis is that some people still think Elvis might be alive!

Dr Kevorkian is the only doctor who ever said, "I did everything I could, but he's still alive."

Some of Dr Kevorkian's patients definitely have grave reservations.

Could you imagine socializing with Dr Kevorkian? Visualize him visiting your house when you didn't feel well, and him asking, "How are you?" And your reply, "Well, I'm (noticing him watching) . . . uh . . . *fine*?!"

To the young, death is a distant rumor, and opportunities are taken for granted on the assumption that they will always be there waiting.

The only difference between sex and death is that with death you can do it alone and nobody's going to make fun of you.   *Woody Allen*

The only way any of us ever die is by suicide.

Do you know how to tell when a central banker's father passes away? The lights dim and, peasants in Italy cross themselves!   *PQ Wall*

I don't know where it's going to stop, except at the end.   *Yogi Berra*

Where there's a will there's a wail!   *Leo Rosten*

I'm not afraid of death. I just don't want to be there when it happens.   *Woody Allen*

A lot of people my age are dead at the present time.
           Casey Stengel

Death: to stop sinning suddenly. *Elbert Hubbard*

When you don't have any money, the problem is food. When you have money, it's sex. When you have both, it's health. If everything is simply jake, then you're frightened of death.   *JP Donleavy*

Men are carried by horses, fed by cattle, clothed by sheep, defended by dogs, imitated by monkeys and eaten by worms.   *Hungarian proverb*

The best way to get praise is to die. *Italian proverb*

What is the world to a man when his wife is a widow?   *Irish proverb*

Debt

One sure way to get back on your feet is to miss two car payments!

There's always something optimistic to appreciate. For example, even if you can't pay your bills, you can be thankful that at least you're not someone to whom you owe money!

It's better to give than to lend because it costs about the same, yet makes you feel better!

What you don't owe won't hurt you!

In America, anybody can have a second house, a second car and a second TV. All it takes is a second job, a second mortgage and a second wind!

Bills travel through the mail at twice the speed of checks!

He who has only nine, but who must have ten, doesn't need a wallet!

Eternity is the time period to the end of the universe, or the time it takes to pay off your mortgage, whichever comes last!

Ah, remember the good old days when we had depressions we could afford!

Those who laugh when they borrow will weep when they need to repay!

Molehills of debt build mountains of worry!

A "deficit" is what you have when you don't have as much as you did when you had nothing!

The United States is three-*trillion* dollars in debt, yet we still have a Treasury Department. Why? Do they go around counting what we *don't* have?

Blessed are the teenagers, for they shall inherit the National Debt!

One is left to wonder why there is so much month left at the end of the money!

Money can't buy everything, which is why there are credit cards . . . that are responsible for the mourning after!

No wonder the credit-card industry is booming – it provides a way to increase people's yearning capacity!

Have you heard about the sign posted in the lobby of a lending company that read, "Ask about our plans for owning your home"?

Go too much in debt and you'll find yourself discredited!

For some, debt has yet to rear its ugly head. Maybe that's why a baby yells when it's born!

It is only by not paying one's bills that one can hope to live in the memory of the commercial classes.
Oscar Wilde

Denial

To most of us, real life is the life we do not lead.
Oscar Wilde

No matter how much perfume you put on trash, it's still going to stink!

Those who choose not to hear, hear less than the deaf!

Nothing has an uglier look to us than reason, when it's not on our side.   *Halifax*

"Denial" can be more than merely a river in Egypt!

Depression

You know you're in trouble when you call a Self-Esteem Hotline, and get put on hold!

Manic depressives are easy glum, easy glow!

A man jumped off the Empire State Building and, halfway down said, "So far, so good."

Depressives' last resort can be to take their favorite beverage to a cemetery, sip on it, and feel that at least they're doing better than everybody there!

A depressed hypochondriac is someone who has no trouble to speak of, and who is like lady seers: both misfortunetellers.

Depression is when you have to face the music, and it's a polka!

Depression is having a mental block, and finding out it's your head!

Misery loves company. As proof, you never see a fly stuck on a fly strip warning other flies to, "Go around! Go around"!!   *Margaret Smith*

Diets

A waist is a terrible thing to mind!

There is a destiny that ends our shapes!

Diets are for people who are thick and tired of it!

I don't want any dessert because I read an article that the Earth is slowing down. So I'm eating less for a while until the spin picks up . . . I'm doing my part!

People will go to any length to reduce their width!

I recently began dating a woman with anorexia, but I'm seeing less and less of her!

Some people have a weight problem – they can't wait to eat!

Just around the time our income reaches the point where food prices don't matter, calories do!

Probably nothing in the world arouses more false hopes than the first hour of a diet. *Dan Bennett*

I met my girlfriend when I hit her with my car. She was very fat. She asked, "Why did you hit me? Why didn't you drive around me?"
I replied, "I didn't have enough gas!"
Rodney Dangerfield

A new study says that over half of all Californians are obese. In fact, half of all Californians are really two-thirds of Californians. *Jay Leno*

Divorce

Why is divorce so expensive? Because it's worth it!

What do you call a recently-divorced woman with three children? A born-again, oral-sex fiend!

Alimony is bounty on the mutiny!

We never know how short a month is until we pay alimony!

He made millions making men's suits, but lost it all making one skirt!

Nobody's perfect: people who marry for love divorce for money, and those who marry for money divorce for love!

He: "Honey, I just hit the lottery and made a fortune, so pack your bags!"
She replied: "Great, Paris? Rome? Where are we going first?"
He: "I don't care where you're going, I'm going where I go. Pack your bags!"

Love is the quest, marriage the conquest, and divorce the inquest!

Many YUPPIES these days are being re-named "DUMPS" (Divorcée Unhappily Making Payments)!

A woman, after she had had fifteen of a man's children, got a divorce on the grounds of compatibility!

A girl said to a man who had recently gotten divorced, "Nice evening, isn't it?" "Um, I'm afraid of commitment." She said: "Good ice cream, want half?" "I don't want half of anything any more." She said, "I'm breathing." And the divorcée fled saying, "Oh, no, not *another* one!"

Some people have the attitude that they're going to bed with their future ex-fiancés!

She got the house, but I got the gate. She got the mining stocks, but I got the shaft. She got half my stuff, but I don't even get half her sex anymore!

The only thing better than marrying a millionaire is divorcing one!

Divorce is no different from a tornado or earthquake – no matter what you do, there's a good chance you'll lose your house!

Alimony is when your former spouse is living beyond your means!

Instead of getting married again, I'm going to find a woman I don't like and give her a house.
Lewis Grizzard

Do you know the definition of the word "alimony"? A man's cash-surrender value!

Paying alimony is like feeding hay to a dead horse.
Groucho Marx

I want there to be one man who will regret my death. *Heinrich Heine*
(bequeathing his estate to his wife on the condition that she get married again)

A second marriage is the triumph of hope over experience. *Samuel Johnson*

Doctors

Old doctors retire. Except for gynecologists, whom women prefer because their hands tremble!

A just-announced survey shows that nine out of ten doctors think that one out of ten doctors is an absolute idiot!

Everybody is worried about crime these days. In fact, I'll never forget the guy wearing a mask who took all my money . . . it was when I was in surgery!

Quacks fill a need, also.

A patient went to his doctor and said, "I have a problem."
"What is it?"
"Um . . . I can't hold my water. I always need to pee. What should I do, doctor?"
"Get off my carpet!"   *Henny Youngman*

Drinking

Labels on liquor bottles these days contain a warning that the contents might harm pregnant women. Which is ironic, since some women wouldn't have gotten pregnant without liquor in the first place!

If only the headache came ahead of the intoxication, alcoholism would be a virtue!

What's the difference between a fox and a pig? . . . Six martinis!

Naturalists who claim America's wildlife is disappearing don't stay up very late at night. America has some fine old ruins, many of which can be seen in our nightclubs. A cocktail lounge is a half-lit room full of half-lit people!

Celebrants should keep in mind that a pink elephant can be a beast of bourbon!

I woke up this morning with a spider in my bed . . . I must have been really drunk last night!

It's the truth that wine improves with age: the older you get, the more you like it!

There's nothing wrong with drinking like a fish, provided you drink what a fish drinks!

How do you know when you have a drinking problem? When you keep asking people for the time, and you can't understand why you keep getting different answers!

Some people use psychics to contact the spirit world and others just use bartenders to become bibulously pixillated!

Where there's a swill there's a sway.

There's no fool like an oiled fool.

My father was never home, he was always away drinking booze. He saw a sign saying, "Drink Canada Dry!" So he went up there.   *Henny Youngman*

The cost of living has gone down a dollar a quart.
W C Fields

Hangover: the wrath of grapes.   *Dorothy Parker*

I always keep a supply of stimulant in case I see a snake. Which I also keep handy.   *W C Fields*

He would have made a very good bartender.
Gore Vidal (on Ted Kennedy)

Often, when you find four subscribers to *The Dines Letter*, you'll find a fifth!

I'm finally getting my first ménage à trois . . . I'm getting screwed by the electric companies and gasoline companies at the same time! But the good news is that now I can drink *or* drive, but I can't drink *and* drive!   *Jay Leno*

Early

The early bird gets the worm, but it's the *second* mouse that gets the cheese!

Because it gets late early.   *Yogi Berra (On why it's so difficult to play left field in Yankee Stadium)*

The worst part about the speed of light is that it makes the mornings come awfully early!

You need to get out in advance, before trouble is obvious. Which reminds me of Sergeant Preston's First Law of the Yukon: it's only the lead dog that gets to see the change of scenery!

If you must rise early make sure you're a bird and not a worm.

Education

Education is something you get when your parents send you to college . . . but it isn't complete until you send your own offspring there!

An economics professor at a college reunion, showed another economics professor his latest exam, who asked, "Isn't this the same as twenty years ago?" He replied, "Yes."
"Don't students pass them on to each other?"
"Yes."
"Don't they all get A's?"
"No. Economics changes every year!"

May is when graduates go to their commencement exercises and are told that the future is theirs. June is when they go to an employment agency and are told the present is *not* theirs!

Tomorrow is today's pupil.

A teacher drills facts, but a great teacher learns.

The dictionary is a poem about everything!

Education is a technique applied to minds so that they can evolve from arrogant certainty, to pensive uncertainty, to naked panic!

Common sense is logic without frills.

It doesn't make much difference what you study, as long as you don't like it.   *Finley Peter Dunne*

His studies were pursued but never effectually overtaken.   *H G Wells*

When a man's education is finished, he is finished.
E A Filene

You aren't learning anything while you're talking!
Lyndon B Johnson

If you think education is expensive, try ignorance!
Derek Bok

We never know the worth of water until the well is dry.   *Eighteenth-Century English proverb*

The primary purpose of a liberal education is to make one's mind a pleasant place in which to spend one's time.   *Sydney J Harris*

I have never let my schooling interfere with my education.   *Mark Twain*

Experience

A parent never wakes up a second child just to see it smile!

We learn from experience that people never learn from experience!

What's the difference between education and experience? Education is what you get from reading the small print in a contract. Experience is what you get from not reading it!

Experience is a wonderful thing because it enables us to recognize a mistake when we make it again . . . and is something we'd be glad to sell for less than we paid for it!

Experience is what you imagine you have until you get more!

There's no fool like an old fool, proving that you can't beat experience!

Experience is what you have left after everything else is gone!

If experience is such a great teacher, how come you never get to graduate?

Experience is what you get instead of what you went after!

Learn from the mistakes of others because you won't live long enough to make them all yourself. And the person who says he's too old to learn probably always was!

Dinesism #41: The Dines Rule of Limbs (DROL) "If you don't use your head, you'll use your feet."

An "expert" is a man from another city, and the further away the city the greater the expert!

There's nothing new in the world except the history you don't know!

Be careful about experts, because an ex is a has-been and a spurt is a drip under pressure!

Experience is what teaches you that you need a lot more . . . because a person becomes wise by watching what happens when he isn't!

Obviously, the best substitute for experience is being 21!

If you don't have time to do it right the first time, you'll definitely have time to do it right . . . the second time!

The shipwrecked man shrinks even from calm waters.

Technology is the science of having arranged life so that one need not experience it.

Time is a great teacher, though it kills all its students!

Experience is not only an expensive teacher, but by the time you get through its school, life is over!

Experience is a good teacher, and considering what it costs, it should be!

One reason experience is such a good teacher is, it doesn't allow any dropouts!

Experience is one thing you can't get for nothing!

Some people profit from their experiences, others never recover from them!

The trouble with using experience as a guide is that the final exam often comes first and then the lesson!

Experience is the name everyone gives to his mistakes. *Woodrow Wilson*

Experience is the comb that nature gives us when we are bald. *Russian proverb*

If we could sell our experiences for what they truly cost us, we'd all be rich!

Family

How do you tell the difference between good mushrooms and bad mushrooms? Feed them to your mother-in-law, and if she drops dead, they're good!

Somebody asked me why my relatives don't travel to visit and stay with me, and my secret is that I borrow from the rich ones and lend to the poor ones, and neither ever comes back!

If your denim pants shrink in the laundry, you might end up with recessive jeans!

A family man is someone who replaces the money in his wallet with snapshots!

A typical American home these days is where the parakeet is taught to talk and the kids are told to shut up!

As you all well know, an earthquake is caused by two massive forces pushing against a fault . . . it's like your wife and your mother-in-law!

Perhaps you're wondering what the difference might be between outlaws and in-laws: outlaws are wanted!

Where there's a will, there's a dissatisfied heir!

Individuals who spend a fortune to have their family tree researched are likely to find that they're the sap. And, like a potato, their best part is underground!

There was once a man who wanted to drown his sorrows . . . but he couldn't convince his family to get into the sack.

Happiness is having a large, loving, caring, wonderful, close-knit family . . . in another city!

George Burns

A man moved into a nudist colony, and received a letter from his mother asking him to send her a current picture. Too embarrassed to let her know that he lived in a nudist colony, he cut one in half and sent her the top part. Later, he received another letter asking him to send a picture to his grandmother. The man cut another picture in half, but accidentally sent the bottom half. He was really worried when he realized that he had sent the wrong part, but then remembered how bad his grandmother's eyesight was and hoped she wouldn't notice. A few weeks later he received a letter from his grandmother. It said, "Thank you for the picture. Change your hair style. It makes your nose look long." *(Encountered on the Internet)*

Fear

Fear is the lengthened shadow of the unknown.

The only thing we need to fear is no fear about fear itself!

Courage is fear that has said its prayers!

Fear is forward. No one is afraid of yesterday.
Renata Adler

Finance

"High finance" is the art of passing money from hand to hand until it finally disappears and goes to "Money Heaven"!

I just heard that gold is weakening in Europe . . . Sam Gold. He's on the 20th day of his honeymoon!

I liked it better when we had folding money instead of folding banks!

In the possible words of Karl Marx's mother, "I wish Karl would accumulate some capital instead of just writing about it."

Investors should think positively, because if their stocks keep dropping, look at all the money to be saved on prune juice. Especially when they say the market is having a "technical correction." That's right, it can tech every nical they've got!

If there's a light at the end of the tunnel, you can be sure someone's going to send you the electricity bill for it!

Ostensibly it's called "take-home pay" because there's nowhere else you can go with it.

Some people make ends meet, but for others the ends can only wave from a distance!

This new invention might be yet another sign of the end of civilization but, what the heck, we might as well invest and cash in on it!

Perhaps nostalgia is the ability to remember yesterday's prices while forgetting yesterday's wages.

Do you know what they're calling former stock-market billionaires now? . . . "Waiter"!

Banks are institutions that urge you to save part of what you earn, and then lend you money so that you could spend more than you earn!

The surest way to make ends meet is to get off your own!

Never trust bankers to get their figures right. If bankers could count, why do they always have six windows but only two tellers?

They call it "cold cash" because it's never in your pocket long enough to get warm!

All progress is based on the universal innate desire on the part of every organism to live beyond its income!   *Samuel Butler*

What happens if you can't pay your bill at an outdoor cafe? Do they throw you inside?
                                    Steven Wright

Food

Dieting is like ordering "Angel-Hair Pasta" . . . and then finding out that Angel was the *busboy*!

Nothing lasts as long as a box of cereal you don't like!

Artichoke: that vegetable of which one has more at the finish than at the start of a dinner.
Lord Chesterfield

There's a new baby food on the market, which is half orange juice and half garlic; it not only makes the baby healthier, but easier to find in the dark!

When the butcher told the lady that his steak cost $20 a pound she complained that his competitor only charged $5 a pound. So the butcher told her to go buy from his competitor. But when the lady replied that the competitor was completely sold out, the butcher said, "If I didn't have any I would sell them for a dollar a pound!"

Have you ever spelled Evian water backwards? That is, for *naive* Americans, it translates as: "Sewer Water, Paris 2001"!

She's such a bad cook that she uses the smoke alarm as a timer!

To impress onlookers, thump a watermelon melodramatically, because if it sounds hollow it will impress them – and they all sound hollow!

You eat what you eat *eats.*

To a sheep, the world is one big salad bar . . . but without the roquefort dressing!

It's actually a fact that, for some celestial reason, an angel shark is sold in restaurants as "monkfish."

Two young German women, tourists in New York, were startled when they saw vendors in New York selling "hot dogs." They were awed that Americans actually ate *dogs.* Wanting however to learn about things American, the pair decided to try them, and sat down on a nearby park bench. One woman opened up the package and screamed to her girl friend, "Ach, so, und vich part of ze dog did *you* get?"

Japanese farmers feed cows beer to make their meat taste better. In the United States, we feed customers beer and they don't *care* how the meat tastes!

Some people are vegetarians primarily because they can run faster than vegetables do!

Peter: The food here is absolutely awful.
Tania: That's true, and the portions are so small!

Remember, when eating in a German restaurant, no matter how bad the appetizer is, the wurst is yet to come . . . But the good news is that you'll always be with the "in kraut"!

Behind every man there's a woman. And behind every Chinese restaurant there's a pile of duck's necks! *Johnny Carson*

Blow in its ear! *(Johnny Carson's reply when he was asked the best way to thaw out a frozen turkey.)*

The most remarkable thing about my mother is that for thirty years she served the family nothing but leftovers. The original meal has never been found.
Calvin Trillin

Age does not diminish the extreme disappointment of having a scoop of ice cream fall from the cone.
Jim Fiebig

No one goes to that restaurant any more; it's too crowded.   *Yogi Berra*

Friends

Before borrowing money from a friend, decide which you need more!

If a friend won't lend you $100, it's probably a close friend . . . Or a relative!

God gave us friends as an apology for our relatives!

You never know how many friends you have until you get a residence near a beautiful area!

Love is blind; friendship closes its eyes.

Best friends are siblings that God forgot to give us.

When it hurts to look back, and you're scared to look ahead, you can look beside you and your best friend will be there.

Funny

If the world laughs at you, laugh right back, because it's as funny as you are. A man who can laugh at himself is truly blessed, for he will always have something to laugh at!

The marvelous thing about a joke with a double meaning is that it can only mean one thing.
Ronnie Barker

During the garbage strike, here's how I got rid of my garbage . . . I gift-wrapped it, left it my car, and they stole it. *Henny Youngman*

There are no new jokes, only new audiences.

Humor is ambush that illuminates!

The best way to cheer yourself up: Cheer everybody else up. *Mark Twain*

When you laugh, be sure to laugh at what people do and not what people are!

Satire sent in jest and received in jest is remembered with rancor.

Nothing serious, nothing funny! *Oscar Wilde*

A proverb is the wisdom of many and the wit of one. *Lord John Russell*

Future

I've seen the future, and I can certainly tell you that . . . it's expensive!

An expert is ostensibly someone who will know tomorrow why things he predicted yesterday didn't happen today!

The future is *always* unbelievable, perhaps blessedly so!

If science discovers how to enable us to live a lot longer, it would be a mind-boggling fast forward to envision a balding Bill Gates. Maybe they'll need single's bars for the "over-100 crowd." A typical pick-up line might be, "Hey babe, nice walker!" If we live to be 300, it might be possible to have been married for 280 years . . . Imagine, spousal murder would become like a traffic ticket, while leaving the toothpaste cap off would be a felony!

He who foresees calamities suffers them twice over!

Maybe there'll be a new technological revolution, but it's nonetheless worrisome that it'll be led by geniuses who can't even figure out how to program their VCRs!

When they start putting answering machines in car phones, what kind of message would they leave? "Uh. Sorry, I'm home!"

The old complaint of yore that, "We can't get good servants any more" has now been transmogrified into, "Our server is down"!

What a wonderful world this would be if we all did as well today as we expect to do tomorrow.

Yesterday is a cancelled check; tomorrow, is a promissory note; today is the only cash you have – so open it wisely.   *Kay Lyons*

Nothing is so good as it seems beforehand.
                                        George Eliot

Precautions must be taken in advance.
                                    Japanese proverb

The future ain't what it used to be.   *Yogi Berra*

Perhaps the best thing about the future is that it only comes one day at a time.   *Dean Acheson*

The present is that part of eternity dividing the domain of disappointment from the realm of hope.
Ambrose Bierce

Gamblers

One thing about gambling: never bet on a sure thing unless you can afford to lose!

Why don't gamblers ask how come casinos make so much money?

Maybe the best way to stop a runaway horse is to bet on it!

As per Mass Psychology, the appearance of gamblers in the stock market should set all investors' alarm bells ringing. Especially for gamblers who bet their rent money . . . it will be a "moving experience"!

It's not what you win, it's what you keep!

Have you learned that no horse can go as fast as the money you bet on him? . . . And even dice is a shaky business!

A man came home after a very late poker game and he was greeted by his nagging, sourpuss wife who said, "And just where have you been all night?" The man said, "I've been playing cards, but that's not important. What matters is that I've lost you to Roger Kaputnik." She screamed at him, "Lost me! How did you manage that?" It was a heartbreaker, he admitted, "I had to fold with a royal flush!" . . . After his divorce, he realized that poker isn't the only game that starts with holding hands and ends with a staggering financial loss!

Casinos stab you in the buck ... and then have you arrested for carrying a concealed weapon!

I bet on a horse at ten-to-one, and it didn't come in until 5 pm!

Gambling is a great way to get nothing for something!

Adam Smith defined humans as, "The animal that bargains." . . . No dogs exchange bones.

Ninety-nine percent of this game is half mental.
Yogi Berra

There are two great pleasures in gambling: that of winning and that of losing.   *French proverb*

The gambling known as business looks with austere disfavor upon the business known as gambling.   *Ambrose Bierce*

Poker is a game of chance ... but not the way I play it.   *W C Fields*

The winner laughs and the loser says "deal."

Some gamblers believe in betting every day, otherwise they might walk around lucky and never know it!

People greedily buy at Tops and fearfully sell at Bottoms for the same reason that there is an Earthquake amusement ride at Universal Studios in earthquake-prone California, based on Mass Masochism and "the secret desire of all gamblers to lose."

Gay

I'm not gay, but the way my social life is going, I'm glad to know it's there.

San Francisco is very innovative. Gay couples couldn't get medical benefits at work, so they went to Mexico and returned as illegal immigrants!

A doctor asked his female patient why she had a "Y" tattooed on her chest, and she informed him that it's because her boyfriend is from Yale. The doctor then sees a young lady with an "H" tattooed on her chest, and was informed that her boyfriend is from Harvard. Finally, the doctor sees a woman with a "W" on her chest, and he declared, "Don't tell me, your boyfriend is from Wisconsin?" And she replied, "No, she's from Minnesota!"

What do you call a lesbian with fat fingers? Well hung!

Society is so wise that when men are arrested for homosexual activity . . . they're sent to jail!

Did you here that Ellen Degeneres died? . . .Yes, they found her face down in Ricki Lake!

For some mysterious reason, it is a modern-urban legend that getting your "socks knocked off" is somehow more pleasurable than getting your "butt kicked," proving that America is facing in the wrong direction!

Have you ever noticed that gays are never burglars? Burglars like to break in quietly, not make a grand entrance!

The Pope said that "same-sex marriage is not natural." Then, he walked away wearing his pointy hat and his dress, off to his normal routine of no sex at all.   *Bill Maher*

Homosexuality is God's way of making sure that the truly gifted aren't burdened by children.
                                                  Sam Austin

The Book of Life begins with a man and a woman and a garden. It ends with Revelations. *Oscar Wilde*

Here's a little tip for you. Don't come out to your father in a moving vehicle.   *Kate Clinton*

That would be like Ellen DeGeneres asking Kathy Lee Gifford if she could be Frank with her!

Golf

A just-married groom, walking down the aisle, told his bride, "I've a confession to make. To be brutally frank, I play golf all the time, I live it, I breathe it and I'm obsessed by it." The new bride thanked him for his honesty and said, "To be brutally frank, I have a confession also – I'm a hooker." He thanked her for her honesty and said, "What you do is, hold your left hand a little higher than your right, with your thumb down here . . ."

One of the quickest ways to meet new people is to pick up the wrong ball on a golf course!

This is the time for foresight. That's what our politicians exhibit . . . but only on the golf course!

A golfer came before a golf-fanatic judge who asked, "Why are you here?" The golfer replied, "Because I beat my wife to death with a golf club." The judge asked . . . "And how many strokes did that take you?"

Old golfers never die, they just lose their balls!

Speaking of golf, I did hit two really good balls last week . . . I stepped on a rake!

Did you hear about the golfer getting a hole in one, but who then keeled over and died? Cause of death? A stroke!

Golf is the game that turned the cows out of the meadows and let the bull in!

I'm too young to play golf!

A man who had been marooned on a desert island for six long years was thrilled to see a beautiful woman rowing toward him. She had flowing locks glinting in the sunlight and wore a diver's rubber suit. Once ashore, she pulled down the zipper on her right arm and asked, "How would you like a smoke?" He asked, "Don't tell me you brought me cigarettes?" He was ecstatic when she pulled out his favorite cigarette, and puffed away with his face engulfed in pleasure. She then pulled down the zipper on her left arm and asked, "How would you like a drink?" He broke into a big smile and asked, "Don't tell me you brought my favorite drink?" She then pulled out his favorite beverage and, as he greedily gulped it down, she could see tears of joy welling up in the eyes of the poor man who had suffered sensory deprivation for six years. Finally, she reached for the zipper below her belt and asked, "How would you like to play around?" This time the marooned man jumped around animatedly and, with his eyes on fire giggled, "Don't tell me you brought *golf* clubs??"

When primitive man beat the ground with sticks they called it witchcraft. When modern man does the same thing they call it golf. *Michael Neary*

A golf ball will always travel furthest when hit in the wrong direction. *Henry Beard*

Gossip

Mass phenomena will race around the world like never before, especially gossips, for whom a secret is either not worth keeping or too good to keep!

The paradox about gossip is that people always talk about things that left them speechless!

There's nothing busier than an "idle rumor."

Some people will believe anything if you tell them it's a rumor!

It's wondrous to behold how rumors without a leg to stand on get around so fast.

If you would avoid suspicion, do not lace your shoes in a melon field. *Chinese proverb*

Gossip is the art of saying nothing in a way that leaves practically nothing unsaid. *Walter Winchell*

Conversation can be defined as when three people stand on the corner talking. Gossip is when one of them leaves. *Herb Shriner*

What is candor to your face is slander behind your back. *Talmud*

As I grow older and older
And totter toward the tomb
I find that I care less and less
Who goes to bed with whom. *Dorothy Parker*

Secret: what we tell everybody to tell nobody.
Ambrose Bierce

Scandal is gossip made tedious by morality.
Oscar Wilde

Wickedness is a myth invented by good people to account for the curious attraction of others.
Oscar Wilde

Health

Have you ever noticed that people seeking exercise who drive to health clubs search frantically for the parking space closest to the door?

I just read a book on communicable diseases . . . and passed it along to some of my friends.

Doctors say that if you exercise you'll add ten years to your life . . . But maybe you'll spend those ten years exercising. And perhaps that's why women's magazines have 50 pages of recipes and 50 pages of diets!

You know you're in trouble when they make you pay your hospital bill before you're admitted!

Did you hear about the hypochondriac who was cured by the doctor simply saying, "Your insurance won't cover it"? . . . Or, who said, "It's the first sign of old age"?

Happiness is good health plus a bad memory.
Ingrid Bergman

What's the difference between a vitamin and a hormone? . . . You can't hear a vitamin!

God sneezed. What could I say to Him?

Henny Youngman

My illness is due to my doctor's insistence that I drink milk, a whitish fluid they force down helpless babies.   *W C Fields*

Many people lose their health trying to become wealthy, and then lose their wealth trying to get back their health. By the time some people realize that good health is everything, they've lost it . . . The relative values of health and wealth depend on which you have left!

Last night I dreamt that I had insomnia!

Coffee increases the risk of heart attacks by 40%. But the bright side is that you won't die in your sleep!

Holidays

New Year's Day

It would be valuable to include in this New Year's resolutions the lessons learned, to make sure that our resolutions not be what goes in one year and out the other!

St. Patrick's Day

What kind of cologne should you wear on March 17th? . . . Scent Patrick!

Halloween

In San Francisco Halloween is redundant!

"Trick or treat" is what kids play on Halloween and retail outlets play the rest of the year!

Life has indeed become much more sophisticated these days. Many years ago it was ghosts and goblins and monsters and witches that scared you on Halloween . . . Now it's the Dow-Jones Average!

Thanksgiving

Keep in mind that the very definition of "loneliness" is two people and a turkey on Thanksgiving!

Thanksgiving is when over 200-million people gorge themselves on turkey dinners, and then turn on the television to watch 22 football players get exercise!

The year has raced by, and it'll soon be Thanksgiving. The Poultry Raisers of America are sending the biggest turkey in the country to the White House . . . Although, the opposition claims he's already there!

Christmas

The three stages of man: he believes in Santa Claus; he doesn't believe in Santa Claus; he *is* Santa Claus!

If your youngster asks how Santa Claus gets into your house, say he comes in through a hole in daddy's wallet!

Christmas is the greatest thing to happen to inventories since matches.

We always get a little choked up looking at a vinyl Christmas tree . . . We realize that poems are made by fools like we, but only chemistry can make a tree!

Christmas has come to mean the time when the public plays Santa Claus to the retail industry . . . And if you're shopping for the perfect gift for "someone who has everything," how about a burglar alarm? . . . Or insurance?

Have you heard about Adolph, the brown-nosed reindeer? He could run as fast as Rudolph, he just couldn't stop as fast!

It seems that the only people who still believe in Santa Claus these days are doormen, janitors, and newspaper-delivery boys! In fact, we've just received our first Christmas card from our answering service; we didn't mind that so much, but it was the business-reply envelope in it!

Hope

If wishes were horses, beggars might ride.
John Ray

Thinking positively is not hope . . . Hope is the most sophisticated form of despair!

There is no eel so small but it hopes to become a whale. *German proverb*

Maybe we'll all feel better after we've given up hope!

Hope is almost always a self-lie.

Don't spoil what you have by wanting what you don't have. And remember what you now have was among the things you only hoped for.   *Epicurus*

Thy wish was father, Harry, to that thought.
Shakespeare

Hunting

A hunter, lost in the wilds of northern Minnesota, screamed at his guide, "You told me you were the best guide in Minnesota." "Yes," replied the guide, "I am. But I think we're in Canada now!"

It's not generally known that the kiwi bird was nearly hunted to extinction for the fruit and shoe polish it provides!

A moose is an animal with horns on the front of his head and a hunting-lodge wall on the back of it.
Groucho Marx

Give a man a fish and he eats for the day . . . teach him how to fish and you get rid of him for the whole weekend.   *Zenna Schaffer*

Immortality

The secrets of immortality will die with me!

Immortality is a fate worse than death!

Biography is one of the new terrors of death.
Oscar Wilde

Time and I against any two.   *Spanish proverb*

Time is that which man is always trying to kill, but which ends in killing him.   *Herbert Spencer*

There is no cure for birth or death save to enjoy the interval.   *George Santayana*

The fear of death keeps us from living, not from dying.   *Paul C Roud*

You are younger today than you will ever be again. Make use of it for the sake of tomorrow.

No young man believes he will ever die.
William Hazlitt

My grandfather lived to be 103-years old. The truth is, nobody knows what's good for you. Every morning he would eat a raw onion and smoke a cigar. And do you know what his dying words were? Nobody knows, they couldn't get near the guy!

Jonathan Katz

Birthdays are good for you – the more you have the longer you live!

Inflation

When inflation gets bad enough it's going to be an insult to tell a woman that she looks like a million dollars. In fact, the way inflation is going, a person with ten-million dollars could live just as well as if he/she were rich!

We can only wish people didn't tell us we look just like we did twenty years ago. So does the dollar!

Inflation is the system whereby if you save long enough to buy something, you can't afford it!

If you've found a penny in the street lately, it was probably a dime when somebody dropped it!

The worshippers of fiat paper money are like engaged couples, that final period in which lovers keep up their pretenses.

Inflation only occurs when somebody passes you a phony twenty-dollar bill . . . and it's the government who passes it to you!

Americans are apparently getting physically stronger: thirty years ago it took two people to carry ten dollars' worth of groceries, whereas today, a four-year old could do it!

I get especially nervous when I'm told "the US dollar will be stable," because you know what's found in stables!

Inflation is an economic situation that occurs when the prices you get look good but the prices you pay look awful. Inflation is when the buck doesn't stop anywhere. Inflation is when you do more for a dollar than a dollar does for you. Thanks to inflation it's costing more than ever to live beyond your means. Inflation has infected everything, including the wages of sin . . . However, despite inflation, a penny for the thoughts of some Congressmen is still a fair price.

Government statistics clearly prove that there is no inflation. That is, if you don't eat, drive, drink or have a residence!

Insults

We award him the Helen Keller Award For Farsightedness!

He writes for the ages, the ages between five and twelve.

I read his writing under the worst possible circumstances: the light was on.

Have you noticed that all the wrong people have inferiority complexes?

Every profession should have at least one King Farouk. Or a Mussolini!

Nobody has a higher opinion of him than we do, and we don't think much of the dirty, rotten little skunk!

He's so short, he can see his toes in the photo on his driver's license!

He's the mad cow of our industry!

As for charisma, his work goes all around the country stirring up apathy!

In a restaurant he studied the menu and then asked the waitress for a "quickie." He did not understand that it was a *quiche*... And the waitress' name was not Lorraine!

Nobody could be rich enough to buy the right to be so wrong!

That person hasn't a single redeeming vice!

He is *la crème de la pond scum!*

His favorite television show was Dynasty . . . he was fascinated with the upper class.

If you haven't thought much about that person lately, you're not alone!

Getting him to say something specific was like trying to nail custard to the wall!

He's the kind of person who always hits the nail right on his thumb!

I'm not going to respond to his put-downs. I've got nothing bad to say about him. Besides . . . there's nothing I could say about him that has not already been said about hemorrhoids!

What would you get if you crossed a pig with him? . . . Nothing. There are some things that even a pig won't do!

Your barber has quite a sense of humor!

Do they sell that suit in your size?

He's a sheep in sheep's clothing!

He's the only person I know who can strut while he's sitting down. And it's his life's work to announce the obvious in terms of the scandalous.

He has not an enemy in the world . . . but none of his friends like him!

He'll be looked back on as a diamond in the rough, who made a meteoric disappearance . . . Proving that a jawbone of an ass is just as dangerous a weapon today as in Samson's time!

Don't be like the efficiency expert who squirted Visine directly on his grapefruit!

Egotism is the anesthetic that dulls the pain of his singular stupidity!

Very impressive for someone who has to write "L" and "R" on each of his shoes!

That group is a few clowns short of a circus!

Some days you're the dog and other days you're the hydrant!

Some days you're the pigeon and other days you're the statue!

It takes him two hours to watch "60 Minutes"!

I'm not saying that that person knows nothing about foreign policy, but he told me that Kaiser Permanente was the permanent leader of Germany!

Some high-tech stocks look so bad that even Anna Nicole Smith is considering acquiring them!

They even said his baby looked just like him, until they turned it right-side up!

I'm sitting in the smallest room in my house. I have his writings in front of me. Soon they'll be behind me!

When you meet somebody they often ask, "How are you doing?" If they reply, "I'm doing *good*." Say, "You're doing *good*? Not *well*, good? Who are you Mother Teresa? Albert Schweitzer? Monica Lewinsky?" Tell them to watch their adverbs around you.

His most-notable achievement is having discovered a new use for old clothes – he wears them!

He can be outspoken, but we've never seen anyone do it.

What he lacks in intelligence, he makes up for in stupidity!

He's so dumb that when he gets amnesia he actually gets smarter!

Sometimes he gets carried away with his own importance . . . but, unfortunately, not far enough.

Let's not be too critical of the tobacco industry; after all, at least they've already discovered a cure for old age!

We all sprang from monkeys, but some people didn't spring far enough!

May the fleas of a thousand camels infest your armpits.   *Arabian curse*

One time he asked me how he could get enough publicity to get his name in the newspaper . . . so I suggested that he shoot himself!

I heard people talking about his last speech and how unpopular he was, when somebody said, "He's his own worst enemy." Whereupon several other people chimed in, "Not while we're around!"

He's a self-made man and worships his creator. But the way he believes in himself is very refreshing in these atheistic days when so many people believe in no god at all. Actually, he's a good man, but his theology is unsound . . . he thinks there's a fourth person in the Trinity. My only suggestion is that he donate his ego to the Harvard School of Medicine!

He once asked me if I had a quarter because he had to phone a friend. So I gave him 50 cents and recommended that he phone all of them . . . Actually, he and I are both very good friends. There's nothing I wouldn't say to his face . . . both of them!

He's in danger of becoming all things to no people!

I've read his work and the covers are too far apart. His writings are nothing to be tossed aside lightly . . . they should be thrown with great force!

It took me a long time, but I finally grasped the gaping flaw in him, which was the insinuation that, had he lived in those days when the world was made, he might have offered some valuable suggestions!

Lost, the arrogant tycoon stopped his expensive car on the country road next to a farmer. "Hey, you, how far to Glenville?"
The farmer answered, "Don't know."
"Okay, so what's the best way to get there?"
Again the farmer thought and said, "Don't know."
The tycoon snapped, "You don't know much, do you"?
The farmer retorted, "I'm not lost!"

I told him to take a picture of his testicles so he'd have something to remember them by if he ever hit me again.   *Bobby Knight*

"Shut up," he explained.   *Ring Lardner*

I took my wife to a wife-swapping party. I had to throw in some cash.   *Henny Youngman*

I bet you didn't know he wrote poetry. He once got a rejection slip for a poem entitled "Why Do I Live?" And the rejection slip he got back was, "Because you sent your poem by mail."

You look like an extra in a crowd scene by Johann Hieronymus Bosch.

His subscribers are apparently addicted to placebos!

He has something every man wants . . . breasts!

The power to ridicule is the power to destroy.

Not since Attila the Hun swept across Europe leaving behind 500 years of total darkness has there been a man like him.

He has a job equivalent to the lookout on the Valdez!

He's as popular as a Buchanan bumper sticker in Mexico!

That's high praise from someone who thinks mashed potatoes is a finger food!

He doesn't know the meaning of the word fear, but, then, again, he doesn't know the meaning of most words!

That person is living in a house that was rejected by the first little pig!

That person needs brain surgery . . . someone please get a proctologist!

If you ask me, he's done for the field what painting-by-the-numbers has done for art!

Tact is the art of stinging without the stinger!

Do you know why he walks around with his fly open all the time? No? . . . It's in case he has to count to eleven!

You can't win a pissing contest with a skunk!
John Malone

Good taste would likely have the same affect on Howard Stern as daylight has on Dracula! *Ted Koppel*

Oh my God. Look at you . . . anyone else hurt in the accident? *Don Rickles,* said to Ernest Borgnine

May we have the pleasure of your absence?
Henny Youngman

I'm sorry we have two disappointments tonight. Robert Redford couldn't make it and, (*name*) could.
Henny Youngman

I'd like to take you seriously, but to do so would be an affront to your intelligence! *Bill Buckley*

He had the sort of face that once seen is never remembered. *Oscar Wilde*

While he was not as dumb as an ox, he was not any smarter either. *James Thurber*

His imagination resembled the wings of an ostrich. It enabled him to run, though not to soar.

Thomas B Macaulay

(Observing the huge crowd at Louis B Mayer's funeral) It only goes to show that when you give the public what it wants, it will turn out.   *Red Skelton*

Some cause happiness wherever they go, others whenever they go.   *Oscar Wilde*

When Jean Harlow was introduced to Margot Asquith, she mistakenly mispronounced the "t" in Margot. To which Mrs. Asquith replied, "The 't' is silent, as in Harlow."

I admire him, I freely confess it. And when his time comes I shall buy a piece of the rope for a keepsake.

Mark Twain

I've just learned about his illness. Let's hope it's nothing trivial.   *Irvin S Copp*

Remember, men, we're fighting for this woman's honor . . . which is more than she ever did.

Groucho Marx

She's afraid that if she leaves, she'll become the life of the party.   *Groucho Marx*

I could eat alphabet soup and shit better lyrics.
          Johnny Mercer (about a British musical)

A poet can survive everything but a misprint.
          Oscar Wilde

Katharine Hepburn runs the gamut of emotions from A to B.   *Dorothy Parker*

Woman: "My, Mr Berra, you look mighty cool tonight."
Yogi Berra: "Thanks, ma'am. You don't look so hot yourself."

I'm not saying he's taken with himself, but at his birthday party he jumped out of his *own* cake!
          Jay Leno

Intelligence

A genius is someone who aims at something no one else can see . . . and hits it!

Thinking is the culmination of all the bother of our bodily functions!

Plan well or you'll be surprised!

The always silent are either very clever or very dumb. But in either case, at least clever enough to make you guess which!

Doing easily what others find difficult is talent; doing what is impossible for talent is genius.
Henri Amiel

We are all geniuses up to the age of ten.
Aldous Huxley

A straight line is the simplest and most trivial example of a curve.   *Albert Einstein*

What a pity human beings can't exchange problems; everyone knows exactly how to solve the other fellow's.   *Olin Miller*

The public is wonderfully tolerant. It forgives everything except genius.   *Oscar Wilde*

I close my eyes to see.   *Paul Gauguin*

Investing/Stock Market

We are born naked and we die naked . . . so stockbrokers are just doing God's work!

Some investors seeking to buy for the "long term" are so old that they shouldn't even be buying green bananas!

What kind of telephone does a nervous stock-market investor carry? A sell-phone!

For some investors, patience is a virtue that takes too long to learn!

We have a Zen philosophy about stocks. Because we've heard of some investors who started out with $1,000,000. And Zen they had $500,000. And Zen they had $50,000!

On Wall Street, if you see a bandwagon, you're too late!

If you're hunting big fleas you must hang around big dogs!

Some investors don't plan to fail – they fail to plan!

In stocks, as in love, we are astonished by what is chosen by others!

Short-term traders might want to consider this: If a rooster were to lay an egg on a V-shaped roof, which way would the egg roll? Neither. Roosters don't lay eggs!

Wall Street is very hygienic; you either clean up or end up taking a bath!

Why do they call it Wall Street when it's always either going through the ceiling or the floor?

The stock market is the only profession for which no preparation is thought necessary!

Investing gives you a lot of exercise by jumping to conclusions, running up bills, stretching the truth, bending over backward, lying down on the job, sidestepping responsibility, pushing your luck, lifting your hopes and running scared! Unfortunately, the trouble with being so physically fit is that you're apt to wear yourself out trying to stay that way!

There is nothing to get investors' attention like reality's swift kick in the shins!

So many people have lost money in this Mad-Dow meltdown that they're beginning to call it the Ow-Jones Average!

Financial genius is everybody during a bull market!

Buy fear and sell greed!

Please bear with me . . . or, bull with me, as the case might be!

Is this bull market really bungee jumping with yarn?

The market will find your weakness, and then try to destroy you with it!

Some people buy stocks for their old age, and if you buy in a bear market, or sell short in a bull market, you'd be surprised how fast you could get there!

Wall Street is the din of inequity!

The stock market ostensibly doesn't care that it's skating on thin ice. Apparently, to the public, it just means that the price of ice will rise!

There's a coffee shop in the Wall Street area serving a "stock-market breakfast" . . . consisting of scrambled nest eggs!

Dinesism #20 (DIBUBBLE): Economic bubbles are invisible to those inside the bubbles!

The stock market starts out as a passion and ends as a habit . . . like husbands!

The proper time to buy is when you're terrified, and to sell when you're thinking of buying a boat!

Beware of those "diversified portfolios," 20% in Utilities, 30% in oils, 50% in electronics, and 100% in hock. Many investors in no-load mutual funds are finally figuring out that the "no-load" refers to . . . their wallets!

Until the Top, bull markets, like Viagra, won't let you down!

A crash is when you go from having a corner on the market to having a market on the corner!

Always keep in mind the wisdom that, in life as well as in stock markets, entrances are wider than exits!

The person who butts his head against the stock market trend soon learns why it's called Wall Street!

Don't expect your mutual funds to protect you because, when investors finally stampede to sell in the next bear market, most funds will be as illiquid as real estate . . . and might decline so fast that investors will arrive at the bottom slightly younger!

Stock markets continue to send investors to join the Coast Guard, where they separate the men from the buoys!

The market has dropped so much that this is the first time Nike stockholders have made less than Nike workers . . . Wall Street has lost so much money that Anna Nicole Smith has nobody left to date . . . In fact Regis has a new show, "Who Used to Be a Millionaire" . . . Did you hear about the Merrill Lynch bull? It's come down with foot-in-mouth disease . . . I ordered a Big Mac yesterday, and it arrived foaming, with blisters on it.   *Jay Leno*

Happiness is a stock that doubles in a year.
                                        Ira U Cobleigh

The safest way to double your money is to fold it in half and put it back in your pocket! *Mark Twain*

Kindness

He who wishes to secure the good of others has already secured his own.   *Confucius*

One good turn gets the whole blanket!

A soft answer turns away wrath.

Do-gooders are compassion fascists!
                                                Rush Limbaugh

Take care that no one hate you justly.
                                                Publilius Syrus

It is better to suffer wrong than to do wrong, and happier to be sometimes cheated than not to trust.
                                                Samuel Johnson

A candle loses nothing by lighting another candle.
                                                Father James Keller

I wear my heart on my sleeve. I wear my liver on my pant leg.   *Steven Wright*

Knowledge

A little knowledge is dangerous, and very few of us are apparently out of danger!

Confidence is suspicion dozing!

You can't get hit by lightning unless you go where lightning strikes!

The mind can absorb only so much as the tush can take!

A thing that nobody believes cannot be proved too often!

Perhaps one should never know how laws, hot dogs and marital decisions are made!

You can't tell a book by its movie!

Tell me his questions and I'll tell you who he is!

You especially know it's a hot summer when the chair you're sitting on gets up when you do!

We know too much for one man to know much.
Robert Oppenheimer

Somewhere, something incredible is waiting to be known.   *Carl Sagan*

Memory is a crazy woman who hoards colored rags and throws away food.   *Austin O'Malley*

The man who does not read good books has no advantage over the man who can't read them.
Mark Twain

Labor

How does a Teamster tell his child a bedtime story? "Once upon a time-and-a-half ago . . ."

Can hookers get laid off?

According to the latest statistics, there are five-million Americans who aren't working . . . and there are even more if you count those with jobs. Tell a joke to your staff; nothing improves a joke more than telling it to your employees.

How long have I been working for my present employer? Ever since he threatened to fire me!

I've got a problem with my eyesight . . . I can't see going to work!

Summer is the time when it's too hot to do the job it was too cold to do in the winter!

The number one problem in our country is apathy. But, who cares?

The only happy people are those whose work would have been their unpaid hobbies.

It seems an executive can't win these days. If he does something wrong he's fired, but if he does something right he's taxed! (We define an "executive" as someone who can take four hours for lunch without hindering production!)

Workers at the mint are going on strike to make less money!

The trouble with unemployment is that the minute you wake up in the morning you're on the job!

The test of a vocation is the love of the drudgery it involves.   *Logan Pearsall Smith*

Work is the curse of the drinking class.
Oscar Wilde

By working faithfully eight hours a day, you may eventually get to be a boss who will work twelve hours a day.   *Robert Frost*

Not to teach your son to work is like teaching him to steal.   *Talmud*

I work for myself, which is fun. Except for when I call in sick . . . I know I'm lying.   *Rita Rudner*

The model agent told the mediocre-looking applicant, "It would take an act of Congress to get you into modeling." The would-be model said, "That's okay with me," as she began to take her clothing off!

Las Vegas

It's easy to spot honeymooners in Las Vegas – the man kisses his wife even when he's losing!

Some resort hotels here in Las Vegas are surrounded by tropical plants . . . mostly outstretched palms!

"How did you like your vacation in Las Vegas?"
"Terrible. I left my glasses at home."
"Uh-oh. Did you have trouble seeing the shows?"
"No, but I spent the first morning playing a stamp machine."

In Las Vegas, they're getting ready to make a movie called "Marriage, Las Vegas Style." It will be short. The women here don't exchange gifts at Christmas, they just exchange husbands!

In Las Vegas, babies are born mumbling, "But it's a dry heat."

I got caught smuggling books into Las Vegas, but I got off . . . Nobody could prove it was a book!

As I got into the elevator in Las Vegas, a little elderly lady was studying the floor numbers. Suddenly, she screamed out, "C'mon seven!"

In Las Vegas, it's only when the plumbing is stopped up do you realize that a flush *is* better than a full house!

What can you say about a city whose sexually-transmitted disease clinics are called "Balls of Fire"?

California is the state that's washed by the Pacific on one side, and cleaned out by Las Vegas on the other!

In Las Vegas a man said to his wife, "Give me the money I told you not to give me." *Henny Youngman*

The way to beat the gambling in Las Vegas is, when you get off the plane, walk right into the propeller.   *Henny Youngman*

Last Words

I'll always remember the last words of my dear old father... they were, "A truck!"   *Emo Philips*

Eulogy is praise of a person who has either the advantages of wealth and power, or the consideration to be dead.   *Ambrose Bierce*

Lateness

A person with a watch knows what time it is, but a person with two watches is never quite sure!

Ah, well, if it weren't for the last minute, nothing would ever get done!

This is the earliest I've ever arrived late!
Yogi Berra

He was always late on principle, his principle being that punctuality is the thief of time. *Oscar Wilde*

Time is a waste of money.   *Oscar Wilde*

I am a believer in punctuality, though it makes me very lonely.   *E V Luca*

For latecomers, the bones.   *Latin proverb*

Indeed, it's better to cop-u-*late*, than never!

Law

If justice triumphs, we'll appeal!

What's the similarity between a trombone player and a lawyer? Everybody's relieved when they finally close the case!

I've only been ruined twice: once when I lost a lawsuit, and once when I won one. That's because lawyers are the only ones for whom ignorance of the law is not punished!

One great flaw in the jury system is that it's a little frightening to know that your fate lies in the hands of 12 people who weren't smart enough to get excused.

A woman who got married for the fifth time and who was still a virgin, explained: "The first time I got married it was to a gynecologist, who just wanted to look. The second was to a psychologist, who just wanted to talk. The third was to a construction contractor, and he never showed up. The fourth time was to a politician, and all he wanted to do was kiss my ass. Next time I'm going to marry a lawyer and for sure I'll get screwed!"

It's almost time to turn back the clocks . . . the Supreme Court is back in session!

I have now turned 50, am going through menopause, and I enjoy a little litigation. It's costly, perhaps, but salutary, and considerably less expensive than keeping race horses or getting married. *Gore Vidal*

Lawsuit: a machine into which you go as a pig and come out as a sausage. *Ambrose Bierce*

This is a court of law, young man, not a court of justice. *Oliver Wendell Holmes, Jr*

Animals have these three advantages over humans: they have no theologians to instruct them, their funerals cost nothing and no one starts lawsuits over their wills. *Voltaire*

Lies

In case of a crash from 30,000 feet, it's a lie for airlines to call their seats "floatation devices" instead of suppositories. Or, in Italian, an innuendo! The stewardess says to tuck your head between your knees . . . presumably to kiss your booty goodbye.

A statistician is someone who can put his head in the oven and feet in the freezer while telling us, "On average, I feel just fine."

The end justifies the jeans!

Nothing makes a fish bigger than almost having been caught!

Actions lie louder than words.

Kids should never lie . . . wait until you're an adult so you can do it more responsibly!

Hypocrisy is the homage that vice pays to virtue!

Don't feed horse poop to the pony!

There's a deception to every rule!

Even if you feed the cow cocoa, you won't get chocolate milk!

In life, a liar's worst punishment is to believe his own lies!

Guilt has very quick ears to an accusation.
Henry Fielding

If you stop telling lies about me, I'll stop telling the truth about you! *Henny Youngman*

I would define that as bovine scatology.
General Norman Schwarzkopf, Jr.

He only lies twice a year: in summer and in winter.
Sholem Aleichem

A lie can run around the world six times while the truth is still trying to put on its pants. *Mark Twain*

Life

We are aboveground a mayfly moment. So make the most of each instant, because you won't get it again until the next Creation!

Indeed, life is a zoo in a jungle!

Life is a bed of ruses!

Let sleeping dogmas lie!

The hardest thing in life is to learn which bridge to cross and which bridge to burn!   *David Russell*

Like tobacco, drugs, food and communism, all addictions lead to nowhere because the surprise is that in life the trip itself is the destination!

Life is too short to be small!

The secret of life resides within two rules: 1) Don't worry about little things. 2) All things are "little"!

Everything in life has consequences. You can never do merely one thing!

In life "expectation" is not a word, it's merely another restrictive limit!

When does life begin, At conception or birth? Neither . . . Life begins when the children go off to school and get married, and the dog dies!

As you slide down the banister of life, may the splinters never point your way!

Enjoy yourself. These are the "good old days" you're going to miss in the years ahead!

Sometimes in life, there's a gap between hearing and listening!

In life, the last time often transits past us innocuously and unnoticed!

The difference between humans and animals is that many animals are born with their eyes closed, which open later, whereas for humans the reverse is true!

Before undergoing surgery, straighten out your life, because you might live!

If you really want to lead a stable life, marry a horse!

In life, every time history repeats itself, the price doubles!

Good times won't last forever, so keep in mind that time is the thief of pleasure!

Despite the high cost of living, it remains popular!

Anyone who says that, "Life is like . . .," doesn't know a damn thing about life.

The measurement of time is a ruler!

If the world were perfect, it wouldn't be.
Yogi Berra

Life is a near-death experience.   *George Carlin*

At high tide fish eat ants; at low tide ants eat fish.
Thai proverb

The best way to judge a life is to ask yourself, "Did I make the best use of the time I had?" I have no regrets.   *Arthur Ashe*

If you don't know where you're going you might end up somewhere else.   *Casey Stengel*

Fear not that life shall come to an end, but rather fear that it shall never have a beginning.
John Henry Cardinal Newman

Get pleasure out of life. As much as you can. No one ever died from pleasure. *Sol Hurok*

Study as if you were to live forever. Live as if you were to die tomorrow. *Isidore Seville*

When making your choices in life, do not neglect to live. *Samuel Johnson*

The difference between a rut and a grave is the depth. *Gerald Burrill*

Love

There are two times a man is thoroughly happy: just after he's met his first love and just after he's left his last one!

A person in love mistakes a pimple for a dimple!

It's better to have loved and lost . . . indeed, a lot better!

The only proper time to use the word "love" is either in tennis or after you've paid for the room!

If love isn't a game, why are there so many players?

Love is blind. Maybe that's why all the world loves a louver!

Sometimes it's magic and sometimes it's tragic!

L-O-V-E spells "love." But C-A-S-H sometimes also spells love!

To remain a woman's ideal a man must die a bachelor!

The way to a woman's stomach is through her heart!

The average man is more interested in a woman who's interested in him than he is in a woman with beautiful legs!   *Marlene Dietrich*

In love, there's always one who kisses and one who offers the cheek!

Love is blind, but marriage is an eye-opener!
                                    Pauline Thomason

Love is that wonderful interval between meeting a beautiful woman, and discovering that she looks like a herring. Love is temporary insanity curable by marriage because it is based on the delusion that one woman differs from another!

Never part without loving words to think of during your absence. It may be that you will not meet again in life. *Jean Paul Richter*

The primary difference between a momentary passion and a lifelong love is that the latter lasts a little longer! *Oscar Wilde*

The fragrance always stays in the hand that gives the rose. *Hada Bejar*

God gave us our memories so that we might have roses in December. *James Ebarrie*

We always believe our first love is our last, and our last love our first. *George Whyte-Melville*

Love: the triumph of imagination over intelligence. *H L Mencken*

A man can be happy with any woman as long as he does not love her. *Oscar Wilde*

Luck

A person must sit in a chair with his/her mouth open for a long time before a roast duck flies in.
                    Chinese proverb

Some people get to the top only because they got stuck in the back of the elevator!

It's bad luck to be superstitious!

When you wish upon a star, keep in mind that it takes 500-million light years to receive your plea!

Happiness comes through doors you didn't even know that you had left open!

Brains are great, but good luck is even better!

Chance favors the prepared mind. *Louis Pasteur*

Luck never gives; it only lends! *Swedish proverb*

Luck sometimes visits a fool, but never sits down with him.   *German proverb*

Watch out when you're getting all you want; fattening frogs ain't in luck.   *Joel Chandler Harris*

How can one deny that all our lives hang by threads of nothing more than luck? A vagrant microbe, an oil slick on the road, an open door, a leak in a gas line, a madman encountered by chance – against these what matters all our painful accumulations of virtue, knowledge, nobility, sacrifice?   *Leo Rosten*

I believe in luck. How else can you explain the success of those you dislike?   *Jean Cocteau*

If fortune smiles, who doesn't? If fortune doesn't, who does?   *Chinese proverb*

That rabbit's foot you carry for good luck wasn't very lucky for the rabbit, was it?   *R L Shay*

Good luck follows in hot pursuit of High States!

Luxury

Maybe the reason that housing hasn't picked up is that too many people build homes on the outskirts of their incomes!

Luxury is an ancient notion. There was once a Chinese Mandarin who had himself wakened three times every morning simply for the pleasure of being told it was not yet time to get up. *Argosy*

Temptations are the desserts of life!

The trouble with owning a home is that no matter where you sit you're looking at something you should be doing!

Never economize on luxuries. *Angela Thurkell*

I can resist everything except temptation.
Oscar Wilde

Marriage

There are many benefits to marriage, such as sex every night... And, if you're lucky, your partner joins in once a month!

I've never been married, but I once tripped and got my genitals caught in a bear trap, so I know what it's like!

What do you call a woman who knows where her husband is every night? A widow!

The argument with your wife you just won is not over yet . . . When the man has the last word, it's probably in his will . . . And the man who thinks he's smarter than his wife has a really smart wife!

Statistically, 35% of all marriages end in divorce – the other 65% fight it out to the bitter end!

Bachelors have no idea what married bliss is . . . but that's also true for many husbands!

A smart husband buys his wife fine china so she won't trust him to wash the dishes!

All men make mistakes, but married men find out about them sooner!

One should always be in love, which is why one should never marry!

A woman was complaining to her girlfriend about the man she was dating, how he spent money recklessly on her, buying her all kinds of things, and asked her friend how she could stop him. Her friend thought for a moment and said, "Marry him!"

At a Las Vegas wedding, the bride was a woman with the fine prospect of happiness behind her. Yet, she wasn't happy, merely triumphant.

After you've been married to him long enough, you can understand every word he isn't saying!

An optimist is someone who believes marriage is a gamble!

Few romances can survive marriage!

A bachelor is a rolling stone that gathers no boss, but wishes he were having as much fun as his married friends imagined he was having!

After playing tennis my partner got undressed and slipped off a pair of women's panties. I asked him how long he'd been wearing them, and he replied: "Ever since my wife found them in my glove compartment."

Why do the bride and groom smile when walking down the aisle? She knows it's the last time she'll give oral sex, and he's smiling because he doesn't know it yet!

I just ended a relationship . . . I got married!

Some men will sit in a boat all day, waiting to catch a fish, then not hesitate to complain if dinner is a few minutes late!

It's been five years and I'm still in love with the same woman . . . If my wife finds out she'll kill me!

It's amazing how easy it is for a man to understand a wife . . . who isn't his!

When a man asked me how to get his wife to stop ignoring him when he spoke, I recommended that he begin talking in his sleep!

Women tend to marry men like their fathers. That's why mothers always cry at weddings!

College is the only vacation a boy gets between his mother and his wife!

Bigamy is having one wife too many; monogamy is the same!

When a man brings his wife flowers for no reason, he'd better have one!

A well-informed man is one whose wife has just told him what she thinks of him!

These days, the mother who remembers her first kiss has a daughter who can't remember her first husband. Nowadays, young lovers take one another for better or worse . . . but rarely for good! With marriage accurately referred to as the forget-me-knot, the modern lament is, "Always a bride, never a bridesmaid"!

The only way to have your husband remember your anniversary is to get married on his birthday!

I got married because I never did like sex . . . I never cheated on my wife because it's bad enough disappointing one woman!

I shouldn't have gotten married. I was very drunk. What I really said was, "Will you carry me?"

What is the easiest way for a wife to cause hearing loss in her husband? Say she wants to have a serious talk with him!

These days we're told that two can live as cheaply as one . . . but only for half as long!

Complaining that teenagers have too much sex these days is useless. And if *marriage* doesn't stop these youngsters, *nothing* will!

Husbands are men who wish they were having as much fun as their wives think they do!

If love is blind, then marriage is like a trip to the optometrist!

Just remember, marriage and mirage have a lot of the same letters!

Marriage is like a besieged fortress, everybody on the inside wants to get out!

A hip daughter watched her mother try on her new fur coat. The daughter said very unhappily, "Mom, do you realize some poor dumb beast suffered so you could have that fur coat?" Her mother looked at her and said, "Hush! Don't talk about your father that way!"

Sometimes we all just want to be alone . . . It's called marriage!

Perhaps the easiest way to be a man of few words is to always respond, "I understand perfectly."

I saw a stockbroker holding up a stock certificate, and he said to another broker: "What do you think of what I got for my wife?" The other broker reflected briefly and said, "Great trade!"

Do you know what it means to come home at night to a woman who'll give you a little love, a little affection, a little tenderness? . . . It means you're in the wrong house, is what it means!

The secret of getting your wife to talk to you is to talk to another woman. (Wives can use this secret also!)

Acting like newlyweds, she eats salads and he continues to pick up his underwear off the floor!

He who gives in when he is wrong is wise, but he who gives in when he's right is . . . married!

It's like a woman finally having figured out the one thing that all men at single's bars have in common . . . They're all married!

The reason there are so many marriages in June is that it's difficult to think in the heat!

He who marries someone for her looks is like someone who buys a house because he likes the paint!

The young man was shocked when the doctor told him he had to give up sex, but was relieved when the doctor recommended he get married so that it would become less frequent gradually!

Have you heard the one about a wife who got a postcard from her traveling husband that read, "I'm having a wonderful time. Wish you were her"?

If our wives don't treat us men as they should . . . we ought to be very grateful!

Marriage is the romance in which the hero dies in the first chapter!

The poor wish to be rich, the rich wish to be happy, the single wish to be married, and the married wish to be dead.   *Ann Landers*

The only charm of marriage is that it makes a life of deception necessary for both parties. *Oscar Wilde*

It was so cold the other day, I almost got married.
                                                    Shelley Winters

There's only one way to have a happy marriage, and as soon as I learn what it is I'll get married again.
Clint Eastwood

Marriage is a great institution, but I'm not ready for an institution yet!
Mae West

A man in love is incomplete until he's married, and then he's finished.
Zsa Zsa Gabor

One can always recognize women who trust their husbands; they look so thoroughly unhappy.
Oscar Wilde

I haven't spoken to my wife in three weeks . . . I didn't want to interrupt her!
Henny Youngman

God created man and, finding him not sufficiently alive, gave him a female companion to make him feel his solitude more keenly.
Paul Valery

To keep your man, always use place mats, never say "No," take one day at a time, communicate constantly, and never leave him alone with your best girl friend!
Lillian Dines

The surest way to be alone is to get married, because the chain of wedlock is so heavy that it takes two people to carry it – sometimes three. Indeed, marriage is just a souvenir of love!   *Oscar Wilde*

Wives are people who feel they don't dance enough.   *Groucho Marx*

Marriage has driven more than one man to sex.
     Peter Devries

The chief reason why marriage is rarely a success is that it is contracted while the partners are insane.
     Dr Joseph Collins

I love being married. It's so great to find that one special person you want to annoy for the rest of your life.   *Rita Rudner*

A man with pierced ears is better prepared for marriage . . . he has experienced pain and bought jewelry.   *Rita Rudner*

A woman who takes her husband about with her everywhere is like a cat that goes on playing with a mouse long after she's killed it.   *H H Munroe*

There is nothing in the world like the devotion of a married woman . . . It is something that no married man knows anything about.   *Oscar Wilde*

If variety is the spice of life, marriage is the big can of leftover Spam.   *Johnny Carson*

He who tells his wife news, is but newly married.
George Herbert

I was married by a judge. I should have asked for a jury.   *George Burns*

The best way to get a husband to do anything is to suggest that he's too old to do it.   *Shirley MacLaine*

Men are my hobby. If I ever got married, I'd have to give it up.   *Mae West*

Opportunity knocks for every man, but you have to give a woman a ring.   *Mae West*

Marriage isn't a word . . . It's a sentence!
King Vidor

Mathematics

Did you know that five out of four Americans have trouble with fractions?

When you long to be young again, think of having to sit through calculus classes!

A 54-year old accountant left a letter for his wife one evening: "Dear Wife: I'm 54 and by the time you receive this letter I'll be at the Grand Hotel with my beautiful and sexy 18-year old secretary."
When he arrived at the hotel there was a letter waiting for him that read as follows: "Dear Husband: I too am 54 and, by the time you receive this letter I'll be at the Breakwater Hotel with my handsome and virile 18-year old boy toy. And, you, being an accountant, would therefore appreciate that 18 goes into 54 many more times than 54 goes into 18."

(Encountered on the Internet)

Middle Age

You've reached middle age when all you exercise is caution, and jumping to conclusions is about the only exercise you get!

Middle age is when you'd do anything to feel better except give up what's making you feel lousy!

The first sign of middle age is when you're at the bridge you were going to cross some day!

Middle age is when your legs buckle and your belt doesn't!

You know you're getting middle-aged when you start giving advice you never followed in your own youth.

Middle age is a great place to be because you don't need drugs anymore . . . you can get the same effect by standing up fast!

He who hoots with the owls at night will not soar with eagles in the morning. So a slow day follows a fast night and life doesn't begin at 40 for those who went 80 when they were 20!

"Like wow" or "sort of like" is *nouveau balding hippie*!

The younger generation doesn't understand us and uses guns; we just had to go to concerts and take drugs!

The prime of life comes between 16 and 60 (depending on the age of the person doing the talking)!

Perhaps the real secret of eternal youth is just lying about one's age. And realizing we won't lust forever!

You don't stop laughing because you reach middle age; you reach middle age because you stop laughing – that's why I say, "Middle age comes at a bad time!"

Time changes all things. For example, when you're young adultery is a sin, but when you're middle-aged it's a miracle!

The transition in life from looking forward to backward, masks the transition from youth to middle age.

Middle age is when your memory is shorter and your stories are longer.

The first sign of middle age is when you can remember when the air was clean and sex was dirty, and when "safe sex" only meant that the car door was locked! Another sign of middle age is when you bend down to tie your shoelaces, and you look around for something else to do while you're down there!

Middle age is when your sweetheart says, "Let's go upstairs and make love," and you answer, "Honey, I can't do both!"

Middle age is when your friends compliment you on your new alligator shoes and you're barefoot!

You know you're reaching middle age when it takes longer to rest than it does to get tired!

You know you're losing it when you start talking to yourself and even you aren't listening.

You're never too old to learn, and what you learn makes you old!

You're as old as you feel, until you try to prove it!

How old would you be if you didn't know how old you were?   *Satchel Paige*

Anyone who says they can remember the 1970s, that settles it, they weren't there!

Mining

There are land mines and gold mines.

What will we have after we've taken all the ore from the earth? Mined-over matter!

In Vancouver, promoters say that the cardinal rule is to "Never, never, *never* drill!"

Money

Money doesn't grow on sprees!

A penny saved is a pocket burned!

No man is a hero to his wallet!

Cash is Aladdin's lamp.

Cash consists of postponed pleasures!

It's almost as difficult to live within an income today as it was to live without one in the early 1930s!

Remember, there are lots of things more important than money . . . but it takes money to buy them!

Money won't buy friends, but it sure makes for some enthusiastic acquaintances!

If germs cling to money, as we're told, maybe we should find out how they do it!

Money talks – it says "goodbye"!

Nothing gets out of hand quicker these days than money!

Virtue has never been as respectable as money!

Eagles on US dollars are proper and correct because they symbolize swiftness of flight!

The kind of wealth most of us need isn't dollars as much as sense!

Verily, one might well ask, what is six inches long, two inches wide and makes men act like fools? . . . Paper money!

Money doesn't talk, it just makes a sonic boom as it hurtles by!

Maybe the reason money doesn't grow on trees is that banks own all the branches!

Money is the only commodity where quantity automatically includes quality!

Money might as well grow on trees, the way it always leaves!

A farmer, suffering from losses in farming, won a huge lottery and was asked what he planned to do with all the money. He replied, "I guess I'll just keep on farming until it's all gone!"

My doctor said I was sound as a dollar, and that scared the daylights out of me!

Money is the price of life!

Money might not buy happiness, but at least it keeps your family from ignoring you altogether!

Money talks, but if you think it listens, just try getting a loan!

Money is also called "legal tender" because when you don't have it, it's rough!

You can tell the economy is fit: look how fast money goes!

Money can be lost in more ways than won!

Dinesism #38 (DIRICHPOOR): Rich or poor, it's good to have a lot of cash! (You can quote us on that!)

Maybe you can take your money with you, but if you spend it now you can keep others from taking it with *them* after they've taken you away!

There's no economy in going to bed early to save candles if the results be twins.   *Chinese proverb*

Today you can go to a gas station and find the cash register open and the toilets locked. They must think toilet paper is worth more than money. *Joey Bishop*

I have enough money to last me the rest of my life, unless I buy something.   *Jackie Mason*

Music

What's the best thing to throw to a drowning guitar player? His amplifier!

Proof that Americans are a tolerant nation is that the originator of rap music died a natural death.

"Mommy! Mommy!", said the little boy. "When I grow up I want to be a saxophone player."
To which his mother replied, "You can't do both!"

Rock Music: hear today, deaf tomorrow.
Leo Rosten

His music used to be original. Now it is aboriginal.
Sir Ernest Newman (on Igor Stravinsky)

It's an actual fact: When a new music arrived, they used the word for "misshapen pearl" by its detractors, the word having been *baroque*!

I love Wagner, but the music I prefer is that of a cat hung up by its tail outside a window and trying to stick to the panes of glass with its claws.
Charles Baudelaire

I like Wagner music better than any other music. It's so loud that one can talk the whole time without hearing what one says. That is a great advantage.

Oscar Wilde

In ballet you see the music and you hear the dance. It's like living out loud with your body. A dancer's entire body has to speak.   *George Ballanchine*

Mystery

Mother: "Stop asking questions. Don't you know curiosity killed the cat?"
Child: "What did the cat want to know?"

How many of you've ever heard the commercial, "Two out of five people suffer from hemorrhoids" . . . Do the other three enjoy it?

Do you also suspect that black holes conceal all the lost keys, locks from public-bathroom stalls and missing single socks in the world?

Old Age

The older you get the better you get . . . unless you're a banana!

Here's a true story: an elderly gentleman shuffled toward George Burns, who was celebrating his 99th birthday at dinner, and said to him, "I'm 80 and I played 3 sets of tennis today."
George Burns slowly took the cigar out of his mouth and said, "When I was 80, I had the clap!"

Who remembers the "good old days," when a juvenile delinquent was a boy who played the saxophone too loud?

To celebrate his 100th birthday, Mr Shtinkelkaser decided to have one last fling. So he went to the Mustang Ranch, creaked out of his car, slowly shuffled down the hall and across the room over toward the madam, frequently leaning on his cane, which the madam watched with bemused contempt. Upon reaching her, the old man demanded in his frail, croaking voice, "I want some sex!" She looked at him with total disgust and said, "You can't have any more sex, you're finished!" He looked at her, startled, and replied, "Really? How much do I owe you?" . . . Then a light slowly dawned on the old man's face and he said, "Hey, wait, you're putting me on." And the madam said, "No, that would be $25 extra!"

Old age is when you've finally learned all the answers but can't remember the questions.

A 90-year-old man went to his psychoanalyst and said that three months ago he'd met a beautiful woman, 28-years-old, fell in love, she moved in with him, and every day she made love to him in the morning, after lunch, and then again at night. The psychoanalyst said, for a 90-year-old man that's wonderful, so what's your problem? The elderly gentleman sighed and said, "Now I can't remember where I live!" . . . Then, later, after he had finally remembered his address, he went back to his psychoanalyst and told him that he was going to marry her. And the analyst said to him, "Are you crazy? Don't you realize that, at your age, sex with a young woman could be dangerous . . . even fatal?" And the elderly gentleman replied, "Well, if she dies, she dies"!

Old age is when you're cautioned to slow down by the doctor instead of the police!

Old age is when "getting a little action" means you don't need to take any fiber today!

Old age is when "getting lucky" means you find your car in the parking lot.

Old age is that time of life when you don't care where your wife goes, just so long as you don't have to go with her.

A married couple went to the doctor, and complained that the first time he made love to his wife everything was fine, but the second time he felt so cold that he shivered. He asked the woman whether she had any idea of what might have caused that and she said, "Yes. The first time was in June and the second time was in December!"

Gravity isn't easy, but it's the law!

A man ran into an old friend that he had not seen for many years but, who, by now, was over 80, and asked him, "So, do you still chase all those beautiful women?"
And the old man replied, "Definitely. But sometimes I forget why!"

Ah, well, being over the hill is better than being under it!

The old are the only people really free enough to refuse an invitation to dinner without giving an excuse. Indeed, the primary advantage of being old is that you don't have to go anywhere.

By age fifty, every man has the face he deserves.
George Orwell

They say life begins at 40, but so does baldness, bifocals, bridge work and bunions.

They say I look "distinguished" . . . that's the last stage before *ex*tinguished!

The definition of an "old-timer" is someone who can remember way back when "Aids" was an antacid sold at the candy counter!

I'm old enough to remember way back when radios plugged in and toothbrushes didn't, when a stocking could hold what a child wanted for Christmas, when inflation was something you did to a balloon, when what passes as juvenile delinquency was settled out of court in the woodshed, and when movies were rated on how good they were rather than who was allowed to see them.

The three ages of man are youth, middle age, and "My, you're looking well."

Three things indicate we are getting old: first, the loss of memory . . . and I can't remember the other two!

One of the greatest freedoms of growing old is the freedom we enjoy from life-insurance salesmen!

Old age is always ten years older than we are!

Old age is a very high price to pay for maturity.

He's been married a long time, 50 years actually. She left him 3 years ago and he doesn't know it yet!

Remember when everybody slept around and did drugs? I really miss those days. I guess I'm just an old-fashioned guy!

Scientists tell us that the universe is ten-to fifteen-billion years old. How can they be sure? They can't even tell Elizabeth Taylor's age!

I've started wearing my underwear higher, at my hips. The older you are the higher you wear your underwear. Like rings on a tree. When I'm 80 it'll cover my breasts. Then, when I die, they can just pull it over my head!

If you lose your memory, forget about it!

By the time you're old enough to understand the opposite sex, they don't notice you any more!

Petroleum actually comes from decomposed dinosaurs, proving that there's no fuel like an old fuel!

At an elderly auction, a man announced that he had lost his wallet with $1,000 in it, and would give a reward of $100 to anyone who had found it. Another one of the bidders piped up and said, "I'll give $200!"

I'm so old I'm grateful for the latest inventions. For example, when I get up at night to tinkle, the light goes on automatically. And when I'm through the light goes off automatically . . . Eventually, I figured out I was going in the fridge!

When a reporter inquired as to whether elderly candidate Bob Dole wore boxer shorts or briefs, Dole replied, "Depends!"

All would live long, but none would be old.
Benjamin Franklin

No one is so old as to think he can't live one more year.
Cicero

We grow neither better nor worse as we get old, but more like ourselves.   *May Lamberton Becker*

The elderly too often live in a typical fry-and-die desert community! *Marcia Fine*

The real trouble with old age is that it lasts for such a short time. *John Mortimer*

You're never too old to get younger. *Mae West*

The secret of staying young is to live honestly, eat slowly, and lie about your age. *Lucille Ball*

I suppose it's difficult for the young to realize that one may be old without being a fool.
W Somerset Maugham

An old man loved is winter with flowers.
German proverb

Young men want to be faithful and are not; old men want to be faithless and cannot. *Oscar Wilde*

In youth we believe many things that are not true; in old age we doubt many truths. *German proverb*

I'm getting old. Sexually, I like threesomes . . . in case someone dies. *Rodney Dangerfield*

A man 70-years old married a spectacularly beautiful 19-year old, and his friends asked, "How did you get such a young beauty to marry you at 70?" He replied, "Easy . . . I told her I was 95!"

The tragedy of old age is not that one is old, but that one is young.   *Mark Twain*

The only good thing about old age is you're not dead.   *Lillian Hellman*

Opportunity

The difference between opportunity and temptation is that opportunity has to knock, while temptation merely has to stand outside and whistle.

Even when opportunity knocks, a person still has to get up off his/her seat and open the door.

How long a minute is depends on which side of the bathroom door you're on.

Your ship can't come in unless you send it out!

Progress is all right, except that it can go on too long!

Procrastination is the grave in which opportunity is buried. However, if the knock at the door is loud and long, it isn't opportunity. It's relatives!

"Someday" is not a day of the week!

Up, sluggard, and waste not life; in the grave will be sleeping enough.　　　*Benjamin Franklin*

I skate to where the puck is going to be, not where it's been.　　　*Wayne Gretsky*

When its time has arrived, the prey comes to the hunter.　　　*Persian proverb*

He who refuses to embrace a unique opportunity loses the prize as surely as if he tried and failed.
　　　William James

Seize the opportunity by the beard, for it is bald behind.　　　*Hungarian proverb*

There are no problems, only opportunities.
　　　General Omar Bradley

When I look back now over my life, and call to mind what I might have had simply for taking and did not take, my heart is like to break. *William Hale White*

Take it easy. That's why they made tomorrow, so we don't have to do everything today. *Barnaby Jones*

Optimism & Pessimism

In every area of life, love whatever you get because that's all you're going to get.

A pessimist always complains about the noise when opportunity knocks!

Always borrow from either cynics or pessimists because they won't expect it to be paid back anyway!

If it weren't for the optimist, the pessimist would never know how happy he wasn't!

The optimist thinks that this is the best of all possible worlds, and the pessimist knows it. A pessimist is a person who has to listen to too many optimists and, when he has the choice of two evils, chooses both!

A truly happy person is one who can enjoy the scenery on a detour!

Pessimists considering turning optimistic would be like giving up their New Year's resolutions for Lent, working on Labor Day, visiting family on Independence day, or finding a butterfly with a tattoo of Cher on it!

One sees the doughnut, the other sees the hole!

Worry often gives a small thing a big shadow, leading some people to burn their bridges before they get to them!

Optimism is contagious, but don't wait to catch it from others – be a carrier!

There are both optimists and pessimists; some people complain because God put thorns on roses, while others praise God for putting roses on thorns!

I was going to buy a copy of *The Power of Positive Thinking*, and, then I thought: what the hell good would that do?   *Ronnie Shakes*

Don't ever look for life to make you happy, start out happy and then bring that happiness to life!

Two wrongs might not make a right, but three wrongs might!

Optimists are people who break mirrors just to make sure they live another seven years!

A pessimist is someone who feels bad when he feels good for fear he'll feel worse when he feels better!

It's not so terrible to be stubborn . . . at least you'll know what you'll be thinking tomorrow.

Pathetically exaggerated enthusiasm perhaps comes from those who support anything they are certain they cannot understand!

Happiness is not always getting what you think you want, although it also could be discovering that that piece of paper under your windshield wiper is just an advertisement!

Never fear shadows. They simply mean there is a light shining somewhere nearby.   *Ruth E Renkle*

A cynic is a man who, when he smells flowers, looks around for a coffin.   *H L Mencken*

Never look back. Something might be gaining on you.
Satchel Paige

Never think you've seen the last of anything.
Eudora Welty

As increasingly cynical as I get, I never seem to catch up!
Lily Tomlin

When one door of happiness closes another one opens; but often we look so long at the closed door that we don't see the one which has been opened for us.
Helen Keller

The blue of Heaven is larger than the cloud.
Elizabeth Barrett Browning

Real happiness is cheap enough, yet how dearly some pay for its counterfeits.

Paradox/Irony

If the world were always logical, men would ride sidesaddle . . . and women's bikes!

We meet our destiny on the road taken to avoid it!

The weakest link in the chain is also the strongest, because it can break the chain!

Strike while the irony is hot!

The reverse side also has a reverse side!

I was planning to be spontaneous, but my plans fell through at the last moment!

Plant carrots in December and you'll never have to eat carrots!

The mind is an amazing thing: it can be totally empty and still not cave in!

The road of excess leads to the palace of wisdom!

The deeper you go the more shallow it gets!

It's like a woman having slept her way to the bottom!

Reality is for people who can't face drugs!

Vincent Van Gogh sent his ear to his girlfriend with a card reading, "Haven't heard from you lately!"

The person who looks too hard for easy work will always go to bed tired!

There is no greater jinx in the world than an organization finally building a monument to itself, or to a person.

Marvel that strip poker is the only game in which the more you lose the more you have to show for it!

Paradoxically, there's no ham in hamburger, quicksand works very slowly, and an alarm clock goes off by going on! And the only thing worse than an alarm clock that goes off is one that doesn't!

A corporation decided to award an annual prize of $10,000 for the best idea for saving the company money, which was won by a young executive who recommended that in the future the prize money be reduced to $1,000!

A desperate need to win is a subtle blunder, paradoxically, and conceals a secret desire to lose!

Yesterday I was walking down the street wearing my eyeglasses, and all of a sudden my prescription ran out.   *Steven Wright*

The Civil War was a conflict that cost more than ten-billion dollars. For less than half, the freedom of all the four-million slaves could have been purchased.
Charles and Mary Beard

Nothing fixes a thing in the mind so intensely as a wish to forget it.   *Montaigne*

Americans adore me and will go on adoring me until I say something nice about them.
George Bernard Shaw

He gets on best with women who best knows how to get on best without them.   *Ambrose Bierce*

Everything is a temptation to the man who fears temptation.   *French proverb*

If men could regard the events of their own lives with more open minds, they would frequently discover that they did not desire the things they failed to obtain.   *Andre Maurois*

If you don't get everything you want, think of the things you get that you don't want.   *Oscar Wilde*

Parents

Remember that the generation who criticizes the younger generation is always the one who raised it!

My dad only hit me once . . . it was with a car!

A man never knows how to be a son until he becomes a father!

It never occurs to a child of 18 that someday he'll be as dumb as his parents are now!

Indeed, adolescence is an embarrassing time of life precisely because that's when everyone's parents turn stupid simultaneously!

The advantage of the emotions is that they lead us astray. Which is why sex must be a sin . . . look at how parents are punished for it!

When my kids give me grief, I figure that's God's way of saying I should've just gotten head!

A boy said to his father, "I'm late for football practice, would you please do my Internet homework for me?" The teen's father said sternly, "Son, it just wouldn't be right." "That's okay," replied the boy, "at least you could try!"

Perhaps when fathers tell jokes, it's just "popcorn"!

Having teenagers is often what undermines a parent's belief in heredity!

Few things are more gratifying in life than observing your children having teenagers of their own.   *Doug Larson*

Be nice to your children. They'll choose your rest home.   *Phyllis Diller*

Parents who demand of their children, "When are you going to get married?" are vulnerable to the retort ... "When are you going to break your hip?"

When I was fourteen, my father was so ignorant I could hardly stand to have him around. When I got to be twenty-one I was astonished at how much he had learned in seven years.   *Mark Twain*

Patience

Persistence is very valuable. There's nothing wrong with falling on your face because you're still moving forward. Don't quit. You'll never know how close you got. Always persist. Never give up. Think of the poor guy who invented Preparation "G"!

Patience is a crucial virtue because you can accomplish almost anything if you have patience: you can even carry water in a sieve if you wait until it freezes!

Never let a computer know you're in a hurry!

Patience is a component of timing, which is a key to happiness.

Perverts

San Francisco is where they have all those *ménages à trois* . I prefer a *fromage à trois:* me, a woman and a piece of cheese!

She's so Southern, she's related to herself!

If a woman of 35 thinks of having children, what does a man of 35 think of? . . . *Dating* children!

Ah, New Zealand. Where men are men, and sheep are . . . *nervous*!

Mary was in the middle of an asthmatic attack, and while she was having trouble breathing, she got an obscene phone call, and he said, "Hey, did I call you or did you call me?"

My buddy is getting older, but he can do things that he couldn't do when he was 20 . . . Such as dating teenage girls! In fact, he once went to jail for something he believed in . . . he believed she was 18!

I've got to leave because I've got a baby sitter waiting: I don't have any children, but where else could you get a 17-year old for only $8 an hour?

A peeping tom is a guy who's too lazy to go to the beach.   *Henny Youngman*

Bush & Cheney, sounds like the name of a chastity belt.   *Arsenio Hall*

True story: did you hear about the shepherd who was shot when a sheep touched the trigger of a gun lying around? . . . Sounds like a lover's quarrel to me!
Jay Leno

Behind every great woman is a man . . . if you're doing it right.
Bill Maher

Pets

Cats are smarter than dogs: you can't herd cats and you can't get eight cats to pull a sled through snow!

Some canine jewelry could give your dog a new leash on life!

Perhaps the real reason dogs are man's best friend is that they don't understand a word we're saying!

I had a cat once . . . kinda tasted like chicken!

Philosophy

I studied philosophy in college. I think . . . therefore I'm single!

Maybe this world is another planet's Hell!

No question is so difficult as that to which the answer is obvious!

I was going to make a joke about existentialism but, I figured . . . why?

A blind man, leaning against a wall, said: "This is the end of the world."   *Greek proverb*

It doesn't matter what temperature a room is. It's always room temperature, right?   *Steven Wright*

Life isn't made to order.   *Lillian Dines*

The phrase "shit happens" is a philosophical bedrock, and there is no answer for it except, "no doubt."

What if there were no hypothetical questions?
John Mendoza

Even the best needles are not sharp at both ends.
Chinese proverb

He who sleeps in continual noise is awakened by silence. *William Dean Howells*

If a painting can be forged well enough to fool experts, why is the original so valuable?
George Carlin

Places

We'll never find intelligent life on other planets. Because if they're really intelligent, they'll avoid us!

Perhaps the reason American cities are so prosperous is that there's no place to sit down!

That place has charms only for those obliged to stay there!

It's been so hot lately that those who are not summering in the country are simmering in the city!

I went to a restaurant there, and the catch of the day was hepatitis!

Arkansas

What are the two biggest lies in Arkansas? "The truck is paid for . . . And I was only helping that pig over the fence, officer."

What's the biggest pick-up line in Arkansas? . . . Nice tooth!

What's the biggest legal issue in Arkansas? . . . When a husband and wife get divorced, do they remain brother and sister?

California

I like California, but the earthquakes shake me up!

In California they grow monsoon crops like rice and alfalfa *in the desert,* and then wonder why they're running out of water!

Canada

Canadians look exactly like Americans, even though they're different. In fact, Canadians are nothing more than unarmed Americans . . . with a health plan . . . who still own shares of Bre-X Mining!

Have you heard about the new cereal called Bre-X? It has vitamins, but no minerals!

Comparing the US and Canada: I understand that in Montreal you're required to be bilingual – in the US, you're not even required to be lingual!

Canada has freezing storms, which really clears out the homeless people . . . and leaves a lot of loose change lying around in the streets!

Why can't a man who lives in Canada be buried in the United States? . . . Because he's not dead!

The Canadian Health Ministry said there was a shortage of sperm, so they would be importing it from the United States. They'll pay $40 a deposit . . . which presumably beats beating the pavement! And I don't like deposits at a sperm bank . . . I prefer the direct type!   *Jay Leno*

When I was crossing the border into Canada, they asked if I had any firearms with me. I said, "What do you need?"   *Steven Wright*

Canada is a country so square that even the female impersonators are women.   *Richard Benner*

Very little is known about the Canadian country since it is rarely visited by anyone but the queen and illiterate sport fishermen.   *PJ O'Rourke*

In any world menu, Canada must be considered the vichyssoise of nations – it's cold, half French, and difficult to stir.   *Stuart Keate*

England

A pedestrian in England asked a policeman why at crossings there were funny beeping sounds, who replied that they inform blind people when it's safe to go. The tourist marvelled, "Wow, in America we'd never let blind people drive!"

France

I was held back at Orly Airport trying to smuggle in some manners!

I hear that business is so bad, and there are so few tourists in Paris these days, that the French have been reduced to being rude to each other.

Los Angeles

In Paris, a perfect-size breast fits into a champagne glass. But in LA it needs to clog a toilet bowl!

Hollywood's best acting job is done by the ex-husband congratulating the man his ex-wife married!

That's as sure a thing as would be opening a store in Hollywood that rented, rather than sold, engagement rings!

The last Los Angeles earthquake was so bad, and the ground shook so hard, that traffic actually moved!

It is said that life begins when the fetus can exist apart from its mother. By this definition many people in Hollywood are legally dead. *Jay Leno*

Los Angeles is a sick place to live. Earthquakes? People aren't scared. Riots? Hey, that happens. Cigarettes? Run for your life! Someone get me a pasta salad and a motivational-cassette tape! *Richard Jeni*

I made a big mistake. Don't ever do it. I bought a very large Thanksgiving turkey in Beverly Hills. And it wasn't until I got it home that I realized it had breast implants.   *Bill Maher*

Miami Beach

Miami Beach is where art deco went to die!

New York

Dying in New York is more than redundant, it's anti-climactic!

The first thing that strikes a stranger in New York is usually . . . a taxicab!

On a New York subway you can get fined for spitting . . . but you can throw up for nothing!

I went to the New York Library and there was a sign: "People are reading quietly, please use your . . . silencer"!

People kid about New York, but all over the world people dream of going there and . . . driving a taxicab!

In certain parts of the world people who play in the streets have accidents, but in New York they're known as "pedestrians."

In New York you can get much more from people with just a kind word . . . and a gun, than you can get with a kind word alone!

Ah, New York, when I drove here this morning, I parked my car, walked two blocks, and encountered my tires on sale!

Camping is not my idea of a vacation. If I had wanted to sleep among bugs and wild animals, I'd go to New York. At least I could go to a nightclub there!

There's no more crime in New York, because there's nothing left to steal!

New York is a wonderful city where something is happening all the time . . . Most of it unsolved!

New York, a city that now leads among the world's great cities in the number of people around whom you shouldn't make a sudden movement.

David Letterman

New York: where everyone mutinies but no one
deserts.   *Harry Hershfield*

San Francisco

In San Francisco, a lady came up to me on the street
and pointed at my suede jacket. "You know, a cow
was murdered for that jacket?" I replied in a psychotic
voice, "I didn't know there were any witnesses. Now
I'll have to kill you too!"   *Jake Johannsen*

Sometimes in San Francisco, traffic is so slow that
if a driver wants to hit a pedestrian he has to get out of
his car to do it!

Did you hear that they've just built a roller coaster
in San Francisco? It's level!

San Francisco has recently seen fires, mudslides,
earthquakes, medflies, sinkholes, snowstorms,
collapsing bridges, electric outages, hurricanic
windstorms, and Willy Brown . . . if we encounter
locusts, we're outta here!

Welcome to San Francisco. But if this is the city
that never sleeps, how come so many people are lying
around passed out? Perhaps the way to solve the
homeless problem would be to let them do jury duty!

Texas

Texas wisdom has it that you should never squat with your spurs on!

A Texan was visiting Israel and was told by a proud farmer that his farm was one-hundred meters by one-hundred meters and he was able to grow some vegetables on it. The Texan boasted that he was a farmer also and that he could drive from dawn until dusk and not reach the end of his property. The Israeli looked sad and said, "That's too bad, I had a car like that once!"

Politically Incorrect

Keep in mind that if there were no divorces, where would we get waitresses?

If a man is walking entirely alone in the woods, and he says something out loud, with not a single woman around to hear him . . . is he still wrong?

It'll be a sad day for sexual liberation when the pornography addict has to settle for the real thing!

Women are really in control, but if they're crazy enough to demand equality, men should keep giving them equality until men really are equal!

Women are "Ms" (pronounced mizz, once considered a charming Southern accent, but now sounding like an angry mosquito). "Man" is a politically incorrect word that has been replaced by "persons," a word so awkward that it is comparable to trying to fit rubber bands on watermelons! When something is bad, they use the word "man," such as for pollution or wars. For example, "Man was responsible for the extinction of the dinosaurs," presumably after he criminally forgot to put down the lid of the toilet seat. It used to be just "Congressman," but now it's Congresswomen for women and Congresspersons for men, having successfully neutered them!

Using the phrase "old man winter" is "politically incorrect," so perhaps we should describe it as heat-disadvantaged climate. We can remember when dogs were just dogs, but now it's politically correct to call them "canine Americans." Why, our memory even goes back sufficiently to remember when you could only die from sex when you were too good at it, such recall possibly ascribable to anchoritic tendencies!

Some "politically correct" definitions are:
bald = persons of skull;
short = vertically challenged;
dumb = hard of thinking;
stupid = logically impaired;
fat = gravity challenged.

A recent hacker is believed to be a woman, which is unusual because they are usually men. And her code words were, "I love you." Even though it caused widespread financial losses and inconvenience, it would have been an even more-deadly virus had she asked the dreaded, "What are you thinking?"
Bill Maher

Men have a much better time of it than women; for one thing they marry later; for another thing, they die earlier.
H L Mencken

A woman never forgets the men she could have had; a man, the women he couldn't. *Augusta Dockery*

He's like Jimmy Carter, but without the charisma . . . described by the politically correct as "charismatically challenged"!

How much fame, money, and power does a woman have to achieve on her own before you can punch her in the face?　*PJ O'Rourke*

If women dressed for men, the clothes stores wouldn't sell much . . . just an occasional sun visor.
Groucho Marx

God made Adam before Eve because He didn't want any advice on the matter.　*Patrick Murray*

I treat the charwomen like duchesses, and the duchesses like charwomen. *Beau Brummell (after being asked the secret of his success with women)*

The years that a woman subtracts from her age are not lost. They are added to the ages of other women.
Countess Diane de Poitiers

Politics

Perhaps the problem with the vast halls of Congress is that they're filled with half-vast politicians!

Our leaders' heads are deeper in the sand than armless clam diggers!

Too bad the only people who know how to run the country are busy driving cabs and cutting hair.

George Burns

Darwin's Theory of Evolution suggests that first came the baboon and then came humans, but politics proves that it could go either way.

Congress continually appoints fact-*finding* committees when what they really need are some fact-*facing* committees!

If you give a politician some facts, he'll draw his own confusions!

Anybody who wants the presidency so bad that he would spend years organizing and preparing for it could not possibly be trusted with the office. But others simply double-cross that bridge when they come to it. Politicians are clear that it is dangerous as a candidate to say things that people might remember.

In the event that some of you think we're being hard on central bankers, we actually can acknowledge them insofar as they bring something extra to their jobs . . . an extra chromosome!

When a reporter approached an elderly politician and asked him what he thought of the abortion bill, he reflected for a moment and said: "Eh, I thought . . . I'd paid it already!"

We must respect the other man's politics, but only to the extent that we respect his theory that his wife is beautiful and his children are smart!

Have you heard about the politician who refused to listen to his conscience? He didn't want to take advice from a total stranger!

A doctor, a physicist and a politician were debating which of their professions was the oldest. The doctor boasted that his was the oldest because the creation of Eve from Adam's rib was medical. The physicist acknowledged that that was true, but before that there was chaos, and only a physicist could have done that. Finally, the politician looked at the other two and declared, "But first somebody had to have created that chaos!"

Now that scientists have gotten the lead out of gasoline, maybe we should give them the names and addresses of a few of our politicians. Maybe we should try to get a law passed where we could sue a successful candidate for breach of promise!

Politics makes strange bedfellows . . . which is how learning to sleep with one eye open was invented!

The politician asked the audience, "And if an airplane carrying the leaders of all our political parties crashed, which then do you think God would have saved?" A little voice from the back of the auditorium querulously queried, "The nation?"

The politician's wife listened to one of her husband's constituents register a complaint, and he said, "You're absolutely right." The politician's wife again listened when another constituent came in and complained about the exact opposite, after which her husband said, "You're absolutely right." After he left, the wife said to her husband, "Why you no-good hypocrite: you told the first person he was right and then you told the second person he was right. That makes you an absolute hypocrite." The politician looked at his wife and said, "You're absolutely right!"

American history is so short that historians have no choice but to get interested in the lives of state governors.

Political science is nothing but recent history, poorly taught!

The function of any American president is to enhance the reputation of his predecessor!

Politicians are bending over backwards to prove their morality. I heard one politician say the other day, "I've never done anything dishonest in my life. All I want from you is a chance!"

Those who admire a rascal do not live in his town!

If the Democrats had wanted Gore to be president so bad they should have voted for impeachment!

Let's hope that President Dubya Bush will remain as resolute as his father was toward broccoli.

Perhaps there is no permanent solution to our political problems, and all we can hope for is relief from the first solutions!

Congress is so strange: a person gets up to speak and says nothing. Nobody listens. And then everybody disagrees!

Do you know the infallible method for knowing when a politician is lying? When he's moving his lips!

Do you know why politicians are so anxious to be reelected? They'd hate to try and make a living under the laws they helped pass!

If Bush couldn't get the economy up in an election year, when could he get it up?

I had hoped Fedhead Alan Greenspan would get a job elsewhere for years; perhaps as a proofreader at an M & M candy factory!

A political platform is like the one on a streetcar: not actually meant to stand on, but just to get on.

The latest dance craze is called "The Politician": it's two steps forward, one step backward, and then a sidestep.

How can political candidates discuss the economy when there isn't any?

All politicians fear high unemployment . . . they fear they might be next!

The experienced politician keeps envy out of his voice when he accuses his opponent of fooling the public!

The way things are going in Washington, some politicians who plan to run for office will be running for cover!

Occasionally, an innocent man is sent to the legislature, but before that many candidates develop straddle sores!

I'm not saying that that politician is old, but if he wins California he'll claim it for Spain!

Dick Morris has written a new book called "Men Are From Mars and Women Are From the Yellow Pages"!

As for leadership, he couldn't direct lemmings off a cliff!

Some overpaid politicians apparently don't even know the difference between roast beef and pea soup: anyone could roast beef!

Keep things as they are, vote for the Sadomasochist Party!

It's not that customs agents are crooked, but they *do* operate under the theory that what you seize is what you get!

It's difficult to look up to a politician who has one ear to the ground!

These days the only time we could be certain that a politician is telling the truth is when one calls another politician a liar!

Political campaigns are when voters find out what a politician stands for, and politicians find out what people fall for!

The way Congress handles the federal budget is like writing a check and having the bank bounce!

Who says Congress spends money like drunken sailors? At least sailors spend their own money!

Politics is a great career . . . unless you get caught!

You can't fool all the people all the time, but our politicians are apparently satisfied with 51%.

"My doctor tells me I've got a bad case of C.R.S."
"What's that?"
"You don't know what C.R.S. is?"
"No."
"Can't Remember Shoot!"

A politician is a person who never met a tax he/she didn't try to hike!

When politicians get to the meat of the matter, it's usually baloney!

It's tough being a politician: you never know when people have stopped following you and started chasing you!

If silence is golden, it's no surprise that those blabbermouths in Congress took us off the gold standard.

Anarchy is the cry of despair that just government is possible.

Why is it when *we're* $1 overdrawn in our checking account it's *our* problem, but when our *government* runs a $200-*billion* deficit it's *still* our problem?

How did the undertaker manage to bury that politician in such a small shoe box? ... They gave him an enema!

Perhaps we can get the president a job as a jester. Then, when he loses the next election, he could say that he's "nobody's fool."

Not only is Washington's face on our money, but now Washington's hands are on it!

The more government in the economy, the less economy in the government!

Governments only act wisely after all other alternatives have been exhausted.

If the government really wanted to save money and improve efficiency, they should continue to pay for the junkets of our Congressmen and Senators, but pass a new law making all the junkets one-way only!

The government is going to be conducting a survey as to why people get bored on the job. Just thinking about that survey makes me drowsy. I guess we don't get as much government as we pay for. Maybe it needs much more pruning and much less grafting. More horse sense and less nonsense. And a government of checks and balances instead of checks and deficits.

Only our government could advocate spending our way to prosperity while it's broke!

To think the Fedhead could seriously improve anything with a quarter-point interest-rate change is an example of governmental arrogance that could only be compared with a mosquito hurtling toward the rear of an elephant with lust in its eyes!

It's a weird world: the strong take away from the weak, the clever take away from the strong, and the government takes away from everybody!

The state is the protection for which you trade curtailment of your freedom?

We recently heard a government official declare that he would "not take advantage" of the public? From where would such love come from?

The primary lesson of history is that we don't learn the lessons of history . . . because most American leaders know as much about history as they do about geography!

It doesn't matter whom you vote for, the government always get in!

Congress doesn't decrease deficit spending because it's awfully hard to get a hog to butcher itself!
                              Senator Strom Thurmond

I don't make jokes. I just watch the government
and report the facts.   *Will Rogers*

Today, if you invent a better mouse trap, the
government comes along with a better mouse.
                          Ronald Reagan

It's dangerous to be right when the government is
wrong!   *Voltaire*

Every revolution evaporates and leaves behind
only the slime of a new bureaucracy. *Franz Kafka*

A government that is big enough to give you all
you want is big enough to take it all away.
                        Barry Goldwater

The art of government consists in taking as much
money as possible from one class of citizens to give to
the other.   *Voltaire*

Government is like a baby. An alimentary canal
with a big appetite at one end and no sense of
responsibility on the other.   *Ronald Reagan*

Were it left to me to decide whether we should have a government without newspapers or newspapers without a government, I should not hesitate for a moment to prefer the latter.

Thomas Jefferson

They who give up essential liberty to obtain a little temporary safety deserve neither liberty nor safety.

Benjamin Franklin

Liberty is the one thing you can't have unless you give it to others. *William Allen White*

George Washington was not merely a man, but a fulcrum who changed the entire future course of the world and universe. Imagine America as having been merely another European kingdom!

I've been criticized for falling asleep during cabinet meetings. I admit it's a serious problem. So much so that it's given me many a sleepless afternoon.

Ronald Reagan

There is no distinctly American criminal class . . . except Congress. *Mark Twain*

Suppose you were an idiot. And suppose you were a member of Congress. But I repeat myself.

Mark Twain

President Reagan asked, "What would this country be without this great land of ours?" *Robin Williams*

Your public servants serve you right.
Adlai Stevenson

Where there are two PhDs in a developing country, one is Head of State and the other is in exile.
Samuel Butler

If presidents don't do it to their wives, they do it to the country. *Mel Brooks*

Political language is designed to make lies sound truthful and murder respectful, and to give an appearance of solidity to pure wind.
George Orwell

The best thing about this group of candidates is that only one of them can win. *Will Rogers*

Poor

If you can blame poverty on the rich, why not blame sickness on those who are healthy?

Mary: What would you do if you found a satchel with ten-million dollars in it?
John: Well, if it belonged to a poor person I suppose I'd give it back!

Money can't buy you happiness, but poverty can't buy you anything!

If I understand economics correctly, there would be no economic problems whatsoever today, if only the poor would just spend more money!

I've never been poor, only broke. Being poor is a frame of mind. Being broke is only a temporary situation.   *Mike Todd*

There's another advantage to being poor . . . a doctor will cure you faster.   *Kin Hubbard*

Problems

An error doesn't become a mistake until there's a refusal to correct it!

The thinking that got us into our problem is not the thinking that will get us out.   *Albert Einstein*

For every problem, there is a solution that is simple, plausible and wrong.   *H L Mencken*

Prostitution

Do you know why Mustang Ranch does not allow female customers? Because if men and women converged at the Ranch, they'd sure lose a lot of business in the waiting room!

I was in Las Vegas and a prostitute approached me and said, "For $200 I'll go to bed with you." So I responded, "Would you pay me cash?"

Psychic

Why do psychics advertise? Shouldn't they be calling *us*?

Yesterday I called a psychic hotline and they said, "Who's calling?" I said, "You don't know?" I said make a prediction... They said your phone bill will be higher next month!

It's like getting a premonition I was going to get a déjà vu!

I stayed up one night playing poker with tarot cards. I got a full house, and four people died.

Steven Wright

Psychology

I once wanted to join Paranoids Anonymous, but they wouldn't tell me where their meetings were!

Ah, well, the good thing about a kleptomaniac is that they can always take something for it!

Does the name Pavlov ring a bell?

When writing to someone, to get their attention, write on the envelope, "check enclosed"!

There are two kinds of people, those who finish what they start, and so on!

There are two types of people in the world: those who divide the world into two types of people, and those who do not!

The difference between "psychoneurotic" and plain-old fashioned nervousness is approximately five-hundred dollars!

The masochist said to the sadist, "Hit me!"
And the sadist said, "Later!"

Psychologists are people who go to striptease shows to watch the audiences!

Sigmund Freud said there was no such thing as a joke. But, then again, how many Austrian comedians are there? I'm afreud some of you are too Jung to appreciate that!

Even paranoids can have enemies!

If you always live with those who are lame, you will yourself learn to limp.

Go to the Paranoid Ward in the hospital, pull open the door and scream, "You!" Everybody will freak out. Someone might whisper, "I've told you for two years he was out there!" The paranoid sees a sign at the mall, "You are here" and says, "Damn, I *knew* that they were watching me!"

Perhaps the best cure for hypochondria would be to forget about your own body and get interested in somebody else's!

Only psychosomatic pain has morality!

There's one bad thing about masochism: you always hurt the one you love!

Hypochondriacs are people who, when they wake up feeling well, call the doctor to find out what's wrong . . . Who exclaim "good grief!" and mean it . . . But the fact is, hypochondria is simply a case of sham pain!

The person who loses his/her head is usually the last one to miss it!

A psychiatrist is someone who asks a bunch of questions that your spouse asks for free!

To share a secret conceals a wish that it not be a secret!

Psychiatry is the care of the id by the odd!

At least a schizophrenic knows how the other half lives!

Schizophrenia beats dining alone.   *Oscar Levant*

Roses are red, violets are blue,
I'm schizophrenic and so am I.   *Oscar Levant*

Tell a man that there are five-hundred-billion stars
in the universe and he'll believe you. Tell him a fence
has just been painted and he has to touch it to find out
that it has been.   *Herb Cohen*

To err is dysfunctional, to forgive co-dependent.
     Berton Averre

After twelve years of therapy, my psychiatrist said
something that brought tears to my eyes. He said, "No
hablo inglès."   *Ronnie Shakes*

Religion

They say Jesus was Jewish, but if that's true, how
did he get a Spanish name? . . . Perhaps Murray Christ
wouldn't have made it!

When somebody tells you that they're born again,
say, "That must have really surprised your mother!"

When a beggar approaches you at an airport, say,
"I gave in a previous lifetime!"

One fish in an aquarium asked another, "Do you think God exists?" The other fish replied, "Of course." The first fish said, "How do you know that?" And the second fish replied, "Obviously, you fool, *somebody* changes the water!"

She was an atheist and so moaned, "Oh my non-existent supreme being!" (She found God later that night!)

Blessed are the pure, for they shall inhibit the earth!

"Quantum mechanics" is the interface between science and the supernatural, especially when it says that they are not even sure time exists – no, not the magazine. But it might mean that atheists don't have a prayer!

Perhaps Hell will turn out to have been an empty theater in which we view our lives as they were on Earth, every moment, on continuous loop, over and over again, forever!

Sunday is the day given over by Americans to wishing they were dead and in Heaven, and that their neighbors were dead and in Hell.   *H L Mencken*

A woman married, and after she'd had 13 children, the husband died. She remarried, and had 16 more children, but this time she died. At her grave, the minister looked skyward and said, "At last, they're together." Somebody asked, "Which husband, the first or the second?" The minister replied, "Neither . . . her legs!"

They have all sorts of new services these days, on the Internet and telephone. Now they've even got a dial-a-prayer service for *atheists* – you dial a number and nobody answers!

What God sends is better than what men ask for.
Croatian proverb

She believed in nothing; only her skepticism kept her from being an atheist. *Jean-Paul Sartre*

There's no such thing as an atheist. Everyone believes he is God. *Allen Ashley-Pitts*

I am never molested when traveling alone on trains. There are just a few words I have to say and I'm immediately left alone. They are, "Are you a born-again Christian?" *Rita Rudner*

Respect

I don't get no respect at all. My mother never breast fed me. She told me she liked me as a friend.
Rodney Dangerfield

I don't get no respect. I joined Gambler's Anonymous. They gave two-to-one I don't make it.
Rodney Dangerfield

I tell ya, I don't get no respect. My kid goes to a private school. He won't tell me where!
Rodney Dangerfield

I called to get the correct time. The recording hung up on me!
Rodney Dangerfield

One woman I was dating said, "Come on over, there's nobody home." I went over . . . nobody was home!
Rodney Dangerfield

I don't get no respect. When I was born the doctor slapped my mother!
Rodney Dangerfield

My wife can't cook . . . in my house the roaches go out to eat! . . . Last night she told me to throw out the garbage . . . so I threw out my mother-in-law!
Rodney Dangerfield

I don't get no respect. Last week the police caught me making love in the back of my car . . . I was alone!
Rodney Dangerfield

We sleep in separate rooms, we have dinner apart, we take separate vacations – we're doing everything we can to keep our marriage together.
Rodney Dangerfield

When I was a kid my parents moved a lot . . . but I always found them. *Rodney Dangerfield*

My first wife was so shy that for ten years she only changed her clothing in the closet . . . After ten years I found out she was banging some guy in the closet!
Rodney Dangerfield

The reward of self-respect awaits at the end of the road of doing the right things!

Reputation is the communal killer instinct, the whip of conformity!

Never idealize others. They will never live up to your expectations. *Leo Buscaglia*

Concerning the statement that no man is a hero to his valet, this is not because the hero is no hero, but because the valet is a valet. *Friedrich Hegel*

Retirement

Before you decide to retire from your job, stay home for a month and watch daytime television!

One wife defined retirement as "twice as much husband, and half as much income!"

Counting your chickens before they're hatched is sensible long-range planning.

The "good old times" – all times, when old, are good. *Lord Byron*

Everything you have wants to own you.
Regina Eilert

Oh! The good old times, when we were so unhappy. *Alexandre Dumas*

Revenge

The best revenge is to live long enough to be a burden to your children.

I went to a restaurant last night and I asked the waiter if there was soup on the menu and he said: "No sir, I just wiped it off" . . . So, I composed myself and asked him, "Do you have frog's legs?" And he looked at me and he said, "No, I just walk this way." . . . I was so amused I burst into the kitchen and yelled "Immigration!"

If thine enemy wrong thee, buy each of his children a drum!

A snooty kid started singing on an airplane, "We're from New York, we're from New York." He asked where I was from and I said, "Under your bed, I'll see you tonight!" . . . The kid stopped singing!

The guy on the flight next to me kept hogging the armrest, so I waited until he fell asleep, I put on the life vest and oxygen mask and shouted in his ear: "We're going down!" It worked . . . And as a bonus he later told me he was no longer constipated . . . and I put my oxygen mask back on!

His neighbor telephoned him at 5 AM to scream at him, "I can't sleep because your damned dog is barking," and slammed the phone down before he could reply. So, the next morning, at 5 AM, he returned the call to that neighbor and said, "I don't have a dog," and slammed the phone down into its receiver!

If we are to abolish the death penalty, I should like to see the first step taken by my friends the murderers.
Alphonse Karr

A man that studyeth revenge keeps his own wounds green.   *Sir Francis Bacon*

Everyone is against using revenge as the motive for punishment. But it sure feels good!

Rich

These days, somebody with ten-million dollars could live just as well as if he/she were rich!

It would be difficult to name someone, anyone, even a single person on this entire planet who would not like to be a millionaire. (But, after a stock-market crash, how about Bill Gates?)

It's not a sin to be rich, it's a miracle!

People once wanted to be rich, but now they seem satisfied just to live as if they were!

It's said that it's harder for a rich man to go through the eye of a needle, but on the news this morning I heard that Donald Trump is building a *humongous* needle!

A society without any rich is certain to be a poor one!

Perhaps it's better to be nouveau than never to have been riche at all!

The wealthy can finally afford to buy all the things they did not have as children. That is, *if* they didn't have children!

The nice thing about having money is that it never clashes with anything you're wearing!

The death of the rich is smelled far away!

Rich has an "enough." How many shoes can one buy, or food, or machines, or any thing or anyone?

He must have killed a lot of men to have made so much money.   *Molière*

The jests of the rich are ever successful.
                                    Oliver Goldsmith

The greatest luxury of riches is that they enable you to escape so much good advice. The rich are always advising the poor, but the poor seldom venture to return the compliment.   *Sir Arthur Helps*

Those who say money can't buy happiness don't know where to shop!   *Gittel Hudnick*

Fools live poor to die rich.   *H G Bohn*

The stingy are always poor.   *French proverb*

Ah, well, the rich might not live longer, but it certainly seems like it to their poor relatives!

Sex

After the act, the man was about to go to sleep when she poked him in the ribs and said, "Women's magazines say that a man should be able to do it four times." The man replied, "At least, with me, you get a good night's sleep."

Two men meet on the street, one looking marvelously California healthy and the other emaciated and weak. The fit-looking soul said, "You look terrible, aren't you getting any on the side?" The pale fellow looked up, startled, and said, "Huh? I haven't had any for so long I didn't know they'd moved it!"

I was standing in line at a drugstore with a shy boy in line standing in front of me. I overheard him ask how much a box of condoms cost. The pharmacist said they were "$9.95, plus seventy-four cents for the tax." The youth mumbled, "Uh, I always wondered how people kept those things on!"

These days there's an argument as to whether or not sex is better than drugs but, clearly, that depends on the pusher!

There are no withholding taxes on the wages of sin.
Mae West

The apparel off proclaims the woman!

You're never too old to yearn!

Chastity is the most unnatural of the sexual perversions!

"Doctor! Doctor! Every time I sneeze I have an orgasm. What should I take?"
"Paprika!", replied the doctor.

It's not the size of the ship, but the motion of the ocean and how long it can stay in port so that all the passengers can disembark!

Nothing risqué, nothing gained!

That's like the peasant girl who became a countess when she went down for the count!

Sex is like money; only too much is enough!

The words "reservoir tip" on condoms sounds completely droll. Is it like the Aswan Dam? Aren't you afraid it might break and contaminate the ground water?

There was a special class at noon on premature ejaculation. But everyone got there early, and by ten they were all gone!

I've had a wonderful fantasy that I made love to three women . . . in the same year!

She's pregnant, but she was so promiscuous she's not even sure it's hers!

I sent away for photographs of beautiful redheads with milky-white skin and luscious red lips . . . so they sent me a picture of Bozo the Clown . . . Then, I ordered a penis-enlarger . . . and they sent me a magnifying glass!

My girlfriend is too wild sexually. The other night she screamed and moaned so loud that it disturbed the neighbors. So I went next door and brought her home!

My wife said men are like buses in that another one comes along every five minutes. And I said women are like New York subways in that you pray to get on and then live in fear!

Sex is something that evolves over the years, from tri-weekly, to try weekly, to try weakly.

Imagine if Earth were named Uranus instead. Woman would be walking around saying, "I wouldn't marry him if he were the last man in Uranus. When you kissed me, it was like Uranus shook. My favorite movie is *Move to the Center of Uranus*"!

At the moment of orgasm, people say, "Oh God" and "Oh baby." To prove that God listens, then they get a baby!

When she said, "You won't respect me in the morning," he replied . . . "So sleep until noon!"

I love talking during sex . . . that's why I've got a huge phone bill!

There's a possible new law requiring places that sell alcohol to also sell condoms . . . talk about one-stop shopping! Let's face it, throw in a pizza, and for some it's a dream weekend!

I don't understand women, I can't even tell when they like me. But I *can* tell when they *don't* like me because of what they say. For example . . . "That's him, officer!"

I slept like a baby last night . . . with a breast in my mouth!

I'm feeling strange because last night I had a sex dream that was so vivid that when I woke up my wallet was gone!

There are no sexual freaks anymore: no matter what it is, there's a magazine for it!

I was out with a girl with 17 rings piercing her ear, so that she looked like a spiral notebook . . . A man with a pierced penis, by adding another hole, could qualify as a flute. If he wore short shorts on a windy day, he could whistle a dandy tune. Dogs would follow him down the street!

I had very limited sexual experience before I got married. On my wedding night I remember I tried to inflate her . . . Then, I asked if *she* enjoyed it!

A man who got up to speak said, "I believe no speech should last longer than the sexual act. In conclusion . . . "

Have you ever made love to someone you didn't care about? . . . They call that masturbation!

A woman wanted sex doggy style, so I humped her leg and peed on the floor. She rubbed my face in it. So I married her!

An elderly gentleman was celebrating his 100th birthday in a nursing home. His friends and relatives wanted to do one last, wonderful thing for him, so they decided to send him a hooker. She burst into his room and declared, "I'm here to offer you super sex!" He paused to consider, and then said to her, wearily, "I'll just take the soup, please!"

There was a knock at the door at 7 AM. I got out of bed and two churchmen stood there wanting to sell me salvation. They asked, "Are we disturbing you?" "Yes, I was having sex." "Oh, you're married." "Don't be stupid, not to a goat." "Surely you're not serious." "Oh no, it's a one-night stand!"

A teacher standing in front of her class asked, "Children, which part of the human anatomy expands twelve times when it's directly stimulated?" Little Mary in the front row started giggling and laughing, trying to cover her mouth with her hand. But in the back row Johnnie raised his hand and the teacher said, "Yes Johnnie?"
Johnnie stood up and said, "Teacher, the iris of the human eye expands twelve times when it's directly stimulated by light."
The teacher said, "Very good Johnnie, that's the correct answer. And, Susie, you have a very dirty little mind, and when you grow up . . . you're going to be very disappointed!"

Always remember that celibacy is *not* hereditary!

Once upon a time, a single man and a married couple were marooned on a tiny island whose main feature was only one tall palm tree. The two men took turns climbing it to search the sea for possible rescuers. Finally, the single man couldn't stand it any longer and wanted some intimacy with the woman, who seemed very interested also. So, one day, while on top of the tree, the single man had an idea, and he yelled down, "Hey you two, stop making love!" The married man was bewildered because he was sitting far away from his wife. The next day, the married man was scanning the horizon from the top of the tree, and looked down at the figures below. He mumbled to himself, "I'll be darned, from up here it really does look as if they are making love!"

A frantic mother screamed into the telephone late one night, "Doctor, doctor, my baby just ate an entire tube of K-Y Jelly! What should we do?" After a moment's reflection the doctor said, "If you really can't wait, call one of the all-night drugstores!"

I once saw graffiti on a condom machine in a men's room that said, "This gum tastes funny."

The difference between sex and love is, sex relieves tension and love causes it!

It was his 100th birthday, and he had been enjoying a 98-year-old, because he was interested in younger women. So he proposed to her, but she said she had some things she had to know before she accepted:
She: I'd like to live in a beautiful place. So where do you live?
He: I have a $5-million condo in Miami.
She: I also like to dress well.
He: I'll give you an American Express card.
She: I like to be taken to the best restaurants, operas and ballets.
He: I'll take you anywhere you want.
She: (Glancing below his belt) And what about sex?
He: (Hesitates) Infrequently.
She: Is that one word or two?

What's the best way to make a bull sweat? Put him in a tight Jersey!

Sex is natural. But not if it's done right.
Woody Allen

When turkeys mate, they think of swans.
Johnny Carson

I've never been lucky at sex. The other night I was going to masturbate . . . *I* had a headache!
Rodney Dangerfield

Do you know what "priapus" is? Doctors know – a man is erect for hours on end. One night a man complained to his wife that he was so erect that he couldn't sleep. So he went to an all-night drugstore, but when he entered he saw a woman behind the counter and, intimidated, was ready to leave – but she beckoned him in and asked what he wanted. He complained that he had had an erection for hours on end, most of each and every day. Then he asked, "So what can you give me for it?" The young lady said she'd have to speak to the pharmacist in the rear, who was her sister. So he waited and waited and waited, and was ready to leave when she reappeared and he again inquired if she could give him something for it. Whereupon she declared, "I was discussing it with my sister and the most we could give you is $20,000 and half ownership in the drugstore!"

Book title: The Solution Is In My Hands!
Peter Gripper

Book title: The Yanks Are Coming! *Jack Meoff*

Nothing stimulates you like a good woman . . . So can a bad woman! *Johnny Carson*

Love is the answer, but while you're waiting for the answer, sex raises some pretty good questions.
Woody Allen

The girl I saw in *Playboy* was amazing. I don't think she had silicon, I think she had helium. She was so big I couldn't keep the magazine closed.

Rita Rudner

Men aren't attracted to me by my mind, but what I don't mind.

Gypsy Rose Lee

Artificial insemination is copulation without representation.

Playboy Magazine

Falsies: hidden persuaders.

Mae West

If a thing is worth doing, it is worth doing slowly . . . very slowly.

Gypsy Rose Lee

Passions are like the trout in a pond: one devours the others until only one fat old trout is left.

Otto Von Bismarck

Call me old-fashioned, but I am a deeply-religious woman. That is to say, I firmly believe that there is something Up There. And I'm sure most women feel the same from time-to-time.

Edna Everage

She's been on more laps than a napkin.

Walter Winchell

The devil finds work for idle glands.
Peter's Almanac

What do I think about the show "Vagina Monologues"?... My God, are they *speaking* now?
Norm MacDonald

Shoppers

Veni. Vidi. Visa. (We came. We saw. We went shopping.)

Some shoppers have no shelf control! The single most-expensive vehicle to operate, by the mile, is the shopping cart!

The fish sees the bait but not the hook.
Chinese proverb

Speeches

I do not object to people looking at their watches while I'm speaking. But I strongly object when they start shaking them to make sure they are still going.
Lord Birkett

After hearing that impressive introduction of me, I thought I had passed away!

If one picture is worth one-thousand words, draw me a picture of the Gettysburg Address!

(Opener) It's a pleasure to see you all here, the big shots, the little shots and those who have just come in from their cocktail hour, the half shot!

(On stage, when you forget what you have just said, declare), "This is why I don't skydive!"

I once went to a seminar where the cocktail hour ran from three to seven, and when I answered questions from the floor, you'd better believe it!

"I often quote myself" George Bernard Shaw once said. "It adds spice to my conversation."

I've heard his speeches 50 times. And I've also enjoyed his joke!

That speaker is so full of hot air that everyone in the audience is likely to leave with blow-dried hair!

The wages of din is laryngitis!

Most speakers are full of single entendres!

Look before you lip!

Useful honesty results in good speeches.

One time he spoke so long, and ran on and on so long, that he apologized that he'd gone far past his time limit. His excuse was that he had left his watch at home. So someone in the audience asked him if he had a pocket calendar!

A speech should be like a woman's skirt: long enough to cover the subject, but short enough to generate interest!

The best speaker is someone who has to catch a plane in twenty minutes!

There are two kinds of public speakers: one needs no introduction, the other deserves none!

The trouble with some speakers is that you can't hear what they're saying, and the trouble with others is that you can. Because some speakers exhaust their audience before they exhaust the subject!

When giving a speech never tell everything you know because some nut in the audience might wake up and demand more!

Some speakers are like the horns of a steer: a point here, a point there, and a lot of bull in between!

There are lots of silver-tongued orators who have the gift of speech, but few know how to wrap it up!

Cutting your speech by fifty percent is half the prattle!

The three secrets of success in public speaking are: be sincere, be brief, be seated!

Sports

It's a well-known fact that the older a man gets, the faster he could run as a boy!

Maintain a healthy positive attitude and keep in mind . . . nothing ventured nothing sprained!

Fishing is nice, if you're in a coma. But watching it on TV is simply stultifying of you!

The fellow who's a good sport has to lose to prove it!

Baseball season starts soon, and it'll be great to see someone grabbing his crotch, other than Madonna or Eminem!

A salesman in a sporting-supply store offered a fisherman some fantastic lures: bright colors, insect imitations, different angles of dangling hooks, with wigglers, buzzers and radars, until the fisherman finally asked the salesman: "Do fish really bite on this stuff?"
The salesman replied: "I don't sell to fish!"

A fisherman walked past a game warden with a huge load of fish. The warden asked how he had caught those fish, so the fisherman took the game warden out on his boat, lit a stick of dynamite, threw it into the water and, after the blast hundreds of fish floated to the surface. When the game warden declared such fishing illegal and started to arrest him, the fisherman lit another stick of dynamite and handed it to the game warden and asked: "Are you going to just talk or are you going to fish?"

There's nothing like horseback riding to make a person better off!

The real reason mountain climbers tie themselves together is to prevent the sensible ones from going home.

Those who knock the ball out of the park can take their time trotting around the bases!

A game ain't over 'til it's over.   *Yogi Berra*

You can't think and hit at the same time.
                                    Yogi Berra

Stupidity

Sometimes when you are arguing with a fool, he's doing the same and people might not be able to tell the difference.

There's one nice thing to be said about stupidity: it gives rise to almost 90% of the world's conversations.

We don't always get paid for what we know but we seldom escape paying for what we don't know!

He who laughs last laughs best, but soon gets a reputation for being slow-witted!

A fool and his money are soon . . . invited everywhere!

You don't learn anything the second time you're kicked by a mule!

He's so dumb he thinks step aerobics is for someone who's lost a parent!

Anybody can make an error, but fools practice them.

A "no-lubrication" act can be as expensive as stupidity!

Stupidity should be painful!

Never play leapfrog with a unicorn!

A store that advertised for a night watchman . . . was burglarized that very night!

He was very proud when he came over to me and said that he had insured his intellect for one-million dollars at Lloyd's of London. So I said, "That's wonderful. And what did you do with the money?"

The self-taught had fools for tutors.

The stupid see stupidity in the faces of genius.

I'm not saying he's dumb, but he once told me that he thought Cheerios were doughnut seeds . . . If you say, "Hi ya, how are you?" he's stuck for an answer . . . So, I'm backing off and only asking him questions I think he could handle, like, how many teams are in the Final Four? Or the color of George Washington's white horse? Or who's buried in Grant's tomb?

The difference between genius and stupidity is that genius has its limits!

Truly, central bankers are so stupid that they must think a condom is a planned-parent hood!

He's so dumb that he thinks Roe *vs* Wade are two ways to cross the Potomac!

Girls have an unfair advantage over men: if they can't get what they want by being smart, they can get it by being dumb.   *Yul Brynner*

Just because the person who criticizes you is an idiot doesn't make him wrong.   *Roger Rosenblatt*

There are no stupid questions, but there are a lot of inquisitive idiots!   *Dr E L Kersten*

Quitters never win, winners never quit, but those who never win and never quit are idiots!
Dr E L Kersten

He who climbs Mount Fuji once is a wise man. But he who climbs it twice is a fool.   *Japanese proverb*

I saw this water-safety manual that actually says that if a shark attacks, you should poke it in the eyes! Who wrote that, The Three Stooges?   *Larry Reeb*

Success

I took a speed-reading course . . . now I can get out of the bathroom in half the time!

If at first you don't succeed, you know enough to avoid skydiving!

Nothing succeeds like excess!

If at first you don't succeed, you'll get a lot of advice!

He who limps is still walking!

Only dead fish always swim with the stream!

When you're on thin ice, safety lies in speed!

The middle of the road is the best place to get run over!

Why is it that the man she gave up to be with you always turns out to have been more successful at something?

The ladder of success might now be an elevator, but it's still self-service!

What's the use of running when you're on the wrong road?

It's easy to find the key to success. The hard part is finding which door it opens!

Never expect to steal third base while keeping one foot on second!

The secret of success is knowing whom to blame for your failure.   *Dr E L Kersten*

When you're getting kicked from the rear it means you're in front. *Fulton J Sheen*

Nothing recedes like success. *Walter Winchell*

Success is a great deodorant. *Elizabeth Taylor*

There are just two rules for success: 1. Never tell all that you know. *Roger H Lincoln*

Success is getting what you want, and happiness is wanting what you get. *Dave Gardner*

Suicide

Suicide is not merely an alternate lifestyle, it is actually a belated agreement with the opinions of one's in-laws.

The only sincere form of self-criticism is the ultimate despair of suicide.

In Sweden, making love to one's wife is considered foreplay . . . Maybe that's why they have the world's highest suicide rate!

A painter can hang his paintings, but we can only hang ourselves!

A 100-year old woman was so depressed that she decided to commit suicide by shooting herself in the heart. Not knowing exactly where it was, she called the doctor for exactly where in her body her heart was located, and he told her it was directly beneath her left breast . . . Unfortunately, she then shot herself in her left knee!

The last telegram sent from the *Titanic* was recently auctioned off. It said, "Help – they won't stop playing Celine Dion's *Titanic* song." And then everyone killed themselves!   *Conan O'Brien*

Taxes

Do you know the difference between a pigeon and a taxpayer? The pigeon can still make a deposit on a Rolls Royce!

Many businesspeople wanted their families to share in the business, but the government beat them to it.

The good news is that the best things in life are free, but the bad news is that the IRS is trying to find a way to tax them too!

IRS! . . . The Income Removal Service!

This is a "land of opportunity," in which everybody has the opportunity to become a taxpayer . . . Patrick Henry ought to come back and see what taxation *with* representation is like!

If Congress can pay farmers not to raise crops, why can't we pay Congress not to raise taxes?

If our president wants to abolish poverty, he could start by abolishing the IRS!

A poor little boy wanted a toy he could call his own, so he wrote a letter to God begging Him to send him $50 to buy one. He mailed it, and a kindly clerk at the post office passed it on to City Hall. It finally reached the mayor, who sent a fifty-dollar bill with an imaginary note from God to the boy. But when the boy received it he exploded in anger and wrote back to God, "Thank you very much for the money, but why did you send it through City Hall? Those bastards keep 50% for taxes!"

A penny saved is a penny taxed!

The IRS wants to legalize muggings!

To paraphrase the Scriptures, the Treasury Department must love poor people – they're trying to create so many of them!

Remember, for us it's taxes, but to the government it's take-home pay!

My neighbor is in trouble with the IRS because they're questioning his deductions for having donated $10,000 to the family of The Unknown Soldier!

My dentist is having a big problem with the IRS; he apparently tried to deduct the tooth fairy as a business expense!

If the meek ever inherit the earth, the IRS would find a way to make them pay inheritance tax!

They're taxing everything and everybody these days; if they tax alcohol, cigarettes and cars any more they're going to lose the entire smoking and drunk-driver vote!

One of the biggest problems in teaching English to foreign visitors is convincing them that "damned" and "taxes" are two separate words!

We heard that a man jumped off the Brooklyn Bridge rather than pay his income tax. That must have been a debt-defying leap!

The thing raised most abundantly in the US is taxes. That's why most Americans are members of the debt set!

Truly, the wages of sin are unreported to all tax authorities!

We're told that the Treasury is buying more dollars to support the dollar. That confuses the public. How does that work? They say to us, "Give me a dollar," which we give to them. Then they pay us back the same dollar we gave. This can't be right. Instead, the government should pay with a Discover card, and that way they could get some money back!

Congress has apparently discovered that it's a lot easier to trim the taxpayers than expenditures, and it's their biggest challenge to extract money from taxpayers without disturbing the voters. Congress must not improve our lot in life any further: we simply can't afford it!

Tax rhymes with tacks, anthrax, lacks, lax, racks, sax, yaks, and heart attacks!

The concept of taxation is simple: you can shear a sheep repeatedly, but you can only skin it once.

On April 15th true Americans can feel bled, white and blue. America is the land of untold wealth . . . just ask the Internal Revenue Service.

We define capital punishment as the income tax!

When it comes to income tax, most of us would be willing to pay-as-we-go if we could only catch up to where we've been!

It took me a long time to figure out the difference between the IRS short form and long form; when you use the short form the government gets your money. When you use the long form, your accountant gets it!

These days, a real patriot is one who says he's sorry he has only one income to give to his country!

The futility of riches is stated very plainly in two places: the Bible and the income-tax return forms.

Imagine the way businessmen feel, as unpaid tax collectors for the government!

America is the only country in the world where it takes more brains to make out the income-tax return than it does to make the income!

We wonder why they call them "tax returns" when so little does!

There are only two kinds of people who complain about excessive taxes – men and women!

The American people can't seem to elect anyone who can keep their promise to cut taxes because, in politics, after all is said and done, a lot more is said than done!

At least there's no danger of today's politicians taxing our imaginations!

More and more people see taxation as a bizarre system in which you spend money, save receipts and somehow come out ahead!

Don't you miss the good old days when Uncle Sam lived within his income and without most of yours? Why can't income-tax forms be more realistic and allow intaxicated taxpayers to list Uncle Sam as a dependent?

Of all the taxes governments impose, the worst is the tax on our patience!

The vice-president was making a speech and said, "Gentlemen, let me tax your memories." Ted Kennedy jumped up and said, "Why hadn't we thought of that before!"

Perhaps the revenge of adults is that we expect modern youth to be strong, courageous and prepared to pay even more taxes than their parents!

Never put off until tomorrow what you can do today; there will only be a higher tax on it!

Always be glad to pay taxes because it means you're making money! Ah, well, paying your taxes goes for a good cause . . . it keeps you out of prison!

The Gross National Product is a federal fertilizer factory!

Death and taxes are always with us, but death doesn't get any worse!

The only people who don't mind getting flu shots are taxpayers . . . because they're used to getting it in the end!

Ross Perot told Larry King that he would fix our tax system by starting with a new, blank sheet of paper!

The one thing that hurts more than paying an income tax is not having to pay an income tax.
Thomas Dewar

At the beginning of the empire, the tax rates were low and the tax revenues were high. At the end of the empire, the tax rates were high and the revenues were low. *Ibn Khaldun (1332-1400)*

Rich bachelors should be heavily taxed. It's not fair that some men should be happier than others.
Oscar Wilde

Television

I find television very educational. Every time someone switches it on, I go into another room and read a good book. *Groucho Marx*

Television has raised writing to a new low.
Sam Goldwyn

Toasts

May you live every day of your life!

Hats off to the past, coats off to the future, and may all your pleasures become habits!

May the happiest day of your past be the saddest day of your future!

May you live in such a way that your memories will be a part of your happiness!

May all your weeds be wildflowers!

May you be the hero of your own life!

Travel

Always travel first class, because if you don't, your heirs will!

In America there are two classes of travel, first-class and with children.

(True story): One time a stewardess told Mohammed Ali that he had to fasten his seat belt before the plane took off. Ali said, "Superman don't need no safety belt."
To which the stewardess replied, "Superman don't need no airplane either!"

A bunch of tourists were viewing Mount Vesuvius. While the guide was going on about the horrendous eruptions in the past, one of the Americans looked over the rim and said to another, "That sure looks deep and hot. Reminds you of Hell, doesn't it?"
Then one European in the group whispered to another, "Those Americans! They've been everywhere!"

Archaeologist: a scientist whose career lies in ruins.

Most people could live within their incomes all year round if they were as economical as they are right after their vacations!

The real problem with your leisure is how to keep other people from using it!

Visits always give pleasure. If not the coming, then the going. *Portuguese proverb*

The man who goes alone can start today; but he who travels with another must wait until that other is ready.   *Henry David Thoreau*

Why spend a lot for luggage? You only use it for traveling.   *Yogi Berra*

It used to be a good hotel, but that proves nothing . . . I used to be a good boy.   *Mark Twain*

My wife tells me she doesn't care what I do when I'm away, as long as I'm not enjoying it. *Lee Trevino*

A friend of mine once sent me a postcard with a picture of the entire planet Earth taken from space. On the back it said, "Wish you were here." *Steven Wright*

Consider the Amelia Earhart Luggage Company, the Ted Kennedy Brake Corporation and the Titanic Deck Chair Company!

The function of travel is to better yourself. How? You'll find out when you travel!

If you spit on the floor at home, we want to make you feel at home. *(Sign in filling-station restroom)*

Instead of the expense and inconvenience of going to Europe, drink a gallon of prune juice while looking at a photograph of the Eiffel Tower by the light of burning $100-bills!

The hollowness of traveling "just to see it," can sublimate into the joy of just being where you want to be.

Did you know that Sanka was the only coffee served on the Titanic?

Trends

We have now switched from the New Deal, Fair Deal, and Square Deal to the Ordeal!

The current bull market, like Ted Kennedy, is staggering!

If the shoe fits, it's out of style!

Many people these days are getting fat removed by liposuction from their rears, then having it re-injected into their faces . . . No wonder Beavis and Butthead are so popular!

Truth

Bragging might not bring happiness, but no man, having caught a large fish, goes home through an alley!

Every dogma has its day!

Truth is not everywhere the same, but real truth is what lasts forever!

Truth is the beginning of the path to creativity!

Transparent aims cast a shadow!

Flattery rarely hurts a man unless he inhales.

All that exists in the universe is truth and resistance to it. Truth is the power of the voice of the universe.

When truth has at last been encountered, there is a mental "click" that is self-audible!

Truth is a treacherous servant!

If you truly want to understand something, try to change it!

Never exaggerate your faults . . . leave that for your friends and children.

A great idea is one that hits somebody else with a bolt of envy!

Jealousy is always deeply-selfish self love, coming from "my loss"!

A closed mouth garners no feet!

Maybe what's wrong with America today is that the word "honesty" is usually preceded by "old-fashioned!"

It's well known that reports by witnesses to the same event can vary widely, so it is fair to wonder about the validity of history such that we are never sure what ever really happened anywhere.

If you want to make people angry, lie to them. If you want to make them absolutely livid with rage, tell them the truth!

Time is the mother of all truth!

One good thing about the truth is that you don't have to remember what you said!

Wit is the truth unleashed naked!

It requires a very unusual mind to undertake the analysis of the obvious. *Alfred North Whitehead*

The truth is more important than the facts.
Frank Lloyd Wright

There are two reasons why a man does anything. There's a good reason and there's a real reason!
JP Morgan

Always be ready to speak your mind, and a base man will avoid you. *William Blake*

If you are out to describe the truth, leave elegance to the tailor. *Albert Einstein*

If one tells the truth, one is sure, sooner or later, to be found out. *Oscar Wilde*

I seem to have been only a boy playing on the seashore, and diverting myself in now and then finding a smoother pebble or a prettier shell than ordinary, whilst the great ocean of truth lay undiscovered before me.   *Sir Isaac Newton*

Never wear your best trousers when you go out to fight for freedom and truth.   *Henrick Ibsen*

Nobody speaks the truth when there's something they must have.   *Elizabeth Bowen*

The power of accurate observation is often called cynicism by those who have not got it.
     George Bernard Shaw

There's a time in the affairs of men to grasp the bull by the tail and face the situation!   *W C Fields*

Obscenity is whatever gives the judge an erection!

When you add to the truth, you subtract from it.
     Talmud

I am conquered by truth.   *Erasmus*

Truth is stranger than fiction because fiction is obliged to stick to possibilities. Truth isn't.

Mark Twain

Something unpleasant is coming when men are anxious to tell the truth.   *Benjamin Disraeli*

I have suffered from being misunderstood, but I would have suffered a hell of a lot more if I had been understood.   *Clarence Darrow*

What flatterers say, try to make true.

German proverb

We can be absolutely certain only about things we do not understand.   *Eric Hoffer*

You should never lie to a woman. Come to think of it, you can't tell them the truth either.

Norm MacDonald

He who says what he likes will hear what he does not like.   *Scottish proverb*

Ugly

You could throw her in the river and skim ugly for three days.

She's so ugly that when she goes into a bank, they turn off the cameras!

Plain women know more about men than beautiful ones do. *Katherine Hepburn*

Her face was her chaperon. *Rupert Hughes*

My girlfriend was ugly. Really ugly. How ugly? She entered an ugly contest and they told her, "No professionals." *Rodney Dangerfield*

Viagra

Viagra is produced by Pfizer, whose motto is, "Viagra is a pill a man can stand up for"!

The Viagra pill that sells for $10 each in the US is going for $80 a pill in Saudi Arabia. Consumers of Saudi oil who thought they were getting screwed by high fuel prices had better really brace themselves now!

Viagra, a drug with great potential – or, impotential!

Will performance anxiety bring a new word into the English language, "viaggravation"?

Will elderly men begin walking around bragging, "I'm on the pill?"

Will women become insecure, as they ask of their partners, is it me, or the Viagra?

Have you heard of the crooks who recently stole a truckload of Viagra? Police suspect hardened criminals!

We're now informed that Viagra may also be taken by women. So will some women just fake taking it?

Does anyone here know which Internet company has just decided to sponsor Viagra? Microsoft!

Viagra is certainly good news for rhinoceri, replacing the pathetically despicable practice of ingesting rhino horns for an illusory virility – albeit adding a new dimension to the word "horny!"

My sex life is good. I tried Viagra. But, boy, they're really strong. The first time I tried one I sprained my wrist. *Rodney Dangerfield*

What's the difference between Niagra and Viagra? Niagra falls!

War

India and Pakistan both now have nuclear weapons. What could be scarier than nuclear weapons in the hands of people who believe in reincarnation?

We would gladly trade all this talk of a new Cold War for a hot peace!

Usually a battle inclines in one direction from the very beginning, but in a manner hardly noticeable. *Karl Von Clausewitz*

War is the lowest form of communication.

Wisdom

The beginning of wisdom is to desire it.

The barrier to arriving at wisdom is its unrecognizability until it's arrived at!

No matter what happens, there's someone who knew it would.

The person who knows everything has a lot to learn. Because it's impossible for him to learn what he thinks he already knows!

Don't try to stem the tide – move the beach!

The more original a discovery, the more obvious it seems afterwards!

A foolish man tells a woman to stop talking so much, but a wise man tells a woman that she is extremely beautiful when her lips are closed!

A good idea has a thousand fathers, but a bad idea is an orphan!

It's impossible to make wisdom hereditary!

Knowledge comes and goes, but wisdom lingers!

Caution is the oldest child of wisdom!

Good wit pounces!

Never make the same mistake twice, or you'll never get around to making all of them!

Indeed, it's getting caught that is the mother of invention!

Life is the tradeoff of youth for knowledge and, hopefully, in some cases, the gaining of "wisdom." Unfortunately, one needs to arrive at wisdom even to understand what it is.

Always study wisdom twice before casting it aside.

Self-knowledge comes in waves and layers.

A rose is a red cliché.

The young man knows the rules, but the old man knows the exceptions.

Wisdom is the teetering on the razor's edge of High States as often as possible.

Curiosity has killed more mice than cats!

Nobody looks at the sun except at an eclipse.
Seneca

The more sand has escaped from the hourglass of our life, the clearer we should see through it.
Jean-Paul Sartre

It's not what you look at, but what you see.
Henry David Thoreau

It's better to be numbered among fools than to be isolated among the wise and to see one's self alone against everyone.   *Molière*

Men can only be happy when they do not assume that the object of life is happiness. *George Orwell*

The chief cause of problems is solutions.
Eric Sevareid

Who is wise? He that learns from everyone.
Who is powerful? He that governs his passions.
Who is rich? He that is content.
Who is that? Nobody.   *Benjamin Franklin*

Wisdom comes by disillusionment.
                              George Santayana

Now that it's all over, what did you really do
yesterday that's worth mentioning?   *Coleman Cox*

Learning without wisdom is a load of books on an
ass's back.   *Japanese proverb*

One finger cannot catch a louse.
                            West African proverb

The juvenile inability to admit wrong is the secret
source of the worst and most-terrible wrongs.

The world is a comedy to those who think, and a
tragedy to those who feel.   *Horace Walpole*

Sometimes the road less traveled is less traveled
for a reason.   *Jerry Seinfeld*

The most important thing in communication is to hear what is being said.   *Peter F Drucker*

I didn't say everything I said!   *Yogi Berra*

Women's Lib

A single man in his forties often has a problem finding a woman at his level of maturity . . . That's why he dates someone half his age!

What's the difference between bonds and men? Bonds mature!

One woman asked her neighbor, "If you're so unhappy with him, why'd you marry him?" The friend replied, "Because a vibrator can't mow the lawn!"

Some people think the larger a woman's breasts, the less intelligent she is. It's actually the exact opposite; the larger the breasts, the less intelligent the *man* is!

Anybody who says this is a man's world is probably not too bright about other things either . . . Even if a man could understand women, he still wouldn't believe it!

Why do men get paid twice as much as women to do the same job? Because women get it right the first time!

Women don't want to hire domestic help these days – so some just marry it!

Behind every great man, there's a woman . . . without enough good clothing!

The average woman would rather have beauty than brains because the average man can see better than he can think!

The United States is the only country in the world where a housewife hires a woman to do her cleaning so that she can do volunteer work at the day nursery where the cleaning woman leaves her child!

Women are definitely smarter than men: women's best friends are diamonds, but men's best friends are dogs. Who got the best of that deal?

One time a man was having an argument with his wife and asked if it wasn't true that male judgment was superior to female judgment. She responded, "Of course dear. After all, you married me and I you."

Every man needs a wife because of all the things that go wrong that can't be blamed on the US Government!

He took his defeat like a man: he blamed it on his wife!

Some women have a terrible memory . . . they remember everything!

Women seem to be all right on bargains until it comes to picking out a husband.   *Kin Hubbard*

A man who guesses a woman's age might be smart, but is not very bright!

The man who boasts that he never made a mistake has a wife who did!

Women's brains are not as smart as men's. Why not? . . . Because they don't have a penis in which to store them!

The problem with a penis is there's usually a dick attached to it!

Teacher: If you had sixteen jelly beans and Jack asked you for ten, how many would you have left?
Mary: Sixteen.

Doctor: "Do you wake up grouchy in the morning?"
Woman: "No, I let him sleep."

When a woman really loves a man, he can make her do anything she wants to!

Women who seek to be equal to men lack ambition!   *Mae Jemison*

Men read maps better than women because only a man can understand the concept that one inch equals a hundred miles!   *Roseanne Barr*

I have yet to hear a man ask for advice on how to combine marriage and a career.   *Gloria Steinem*

I know what men really want. All they really, really, *really* want is someone they can be close to, provided she leaves them alone!   *Elayne Boosler*

I love being single. It's almost like being rich.
                                                Sue Grafton

Men play the game; women know the score.
Roger Woddis

Only choose in marriage a woman whom you would choose as a friend if she were a man.
Joseph Joubert

In the sex war, thoughtlessness is the weapon of the male, vindictiveness of the female. *Cyril Connolly*

Anyone who says he can see through women, is missing a lot.   *Groucho Marx*

I think it can be stated without denial that no man ever saw a man he would be willing to marry if he were a woman.   *George Gibbs*

Like Joan of Arc, my life ended at 19. In my case, I got married.   *Shannon Ireland*

My grandmother was a very tough lady. She buried three husbands. Two of them were just napping.
Rita Rudner

Women are never disarmed by compliments. Men always are. That is the difference between the sexes.
Oscar Wilde

Men don't realize that women are their greatest underdeveloped asset!

There are many more people trying to meet the right person than to become the right person.
Gloria Steinem

My husband said he needed more space. So I locked him outside.
Roseanne Barr

The only time a woman has a true orgasm is when she's shopping.
Joan Rivers

I like a man with brains in both heads.
Let's Talk About Sex (Movie)

Youth

A teenager is someone who is an expert on everything that he doesn't need to study!

Maybe the reason that teenagers know all the answers is that they haven't heard all the questions yet!

Maturity begins to come to youth at the same instant they pay their first legal fees!

Teenagers haven't changed much; they still grow up, leave home, get married and have children; the big difference is that today they don't always do it in that order!

It's easy for the young to make a friend. What's hard is to make a stranger!

Youth is that brief moment in time where in charming innocence they still think that life will work out as they expect!

Did you know that the number-two cause of death among teenagers in the US is guns? Did you know the number-one cause? Not *having* a gun!

Youth was wasted on the young, but maturity was wasted on the old!

Each year takes from our soul and adds something else.

You know your kids are growing up when your daughter starts putting on lipstick and your son starts wiping it off!

The young are the only critics with enough experience to judge my work.   *Oscar Wilde*

Kids these days insist on realistic toys, which is why they've got a gun that shoots real bullets, they've got a bow that shoots real arrows . . . and they've got a junkie doll that really shoots.

The problems of the world are so complex these days that even teenagers don't have all the answers!

As Miss America, my goal is to bring peace to the entire world . . . and then to get my own apartment.
Jay Leno

It's the mistake of youth to think imagination is a substitute for experience; it's the mistake of age to think experience a substitute for intelligence.

Even the youngest among us is not infallible.
Benjamin Jowett

Youth measures in only one direction, from things as they are, to an ideal of what things ought to be. The old measure things as they are, against the past they remember.　　　　*Archibald Cox*

The majority of men employ the first part of life in making the rest miserable.　　　*Jean de la Bruyère*

To be adult is to be alone.　　　　*Jean Rostand*

You've got to do your own growing, no matter how tall your grandfather was.   *Irish proverb*

Bad habits are easier to abandon today than tomorrow.   *Jewish proverb*

It is the malady of our age that the young are so busy teaching us that they have no time left to learn.
                                        Eric Hoffer

The old believe everything, the middle-aged suspect everything, the young know everything.
                                        Oscar Wilde

Remember that when you are a teenager you are in the last stage of your life when you will be happy to hear that the phone is for you.   *Fran Leibowitz*

Extra Bonus! 211 Oxymorons!

An oxymoron is a pair of words that is inherently contradictory. We've put together this small list for your possible edification/amusement:

act natural
affordable housing
air quality
airline safety
alleged confession
anarchists unite!
armand hammer
assisted suicide
balanced budget
beer connoisseur
bittersweet
blue-chip Internets
bond volatility
boxing ring
bureaucratic initiative
campaign promise
casual dress
civil disobedience
civil war
clean kill
clean politics
coerced volunteerism
collective wisdom
college culture
communist entrepreneur

compassionate capitalism
Congressional frugality
Congressional action
consensual crime
conservative communist
conservative libertarian
conventional wisdom
corporate culture
criminal character
death benefits
deficit spending
democratic socialism
dirty money
drug culture
dry rot
dry beer
easy money
efficient government
ethical hacker
exercise restraint
extrapolative thinking
extreme conservatives
extremely moderate
fair taxes
fast food

Fed thinking
Federal Reserve
Federal Express
filthy rich
final rough-draft
fiscal restraint
flat growth
foxy grandma
free agent
free time
free love
fresh frozen
friendly fire
friendly divorce
frozen fries
full-service discount-broker
funny money
fur fashion
fuzzy logic
gang peace
good child
government service
government security
gross income
growth recession
grunge fashion
gun safety
gunboat diplomacy
happily married
happy children
hard dollar
harmless pesticides

healthy tan
holy war
hot chili
human intelligence
humble comedian
illiteracy pamphlet
innocent children
intellectual work
intelligent life
intelligent drummer
Internal Revenue "Service"
intimate homicide
job security
jumbo shrimp
junk bond
last frontier
leisure suit
liberation army
libertarian regulations
like wow
low-risk investing
managed competition
market socialism
mass customization
Mideast peace
military intelligence
moderately extreme
Moscow nightlife
negative growth
negative savings
negative inflation
neutral reaction

new tax
nice punching
non-working mother
normal cheating
obscene profits
obscenely rich
old news
organized government
organized labor
organized crime
original copy
paraphrase literally
peace force
perfectly awful
petty cash
plastic money
pleasurable parenting
political party
political science
political culture
political class
political guts
politically correct
popular culture
popular taste
postal service
pragmatic optimism
presidential leadership
pretentiously humble
pretty disgusting
pretty ugly
progressive flat tax

prudent government
psychedelic culture
rap music
really real
reasonable fees
reasonable inflation
recorded live
resident aliens
respected economist
responsible press
reverse discrimination
revolutionary justice
rush hour
safe sex
safe firecrackers
safe pesticides
savings & loan thrift
science fiction
second best
serious comedy
small crowd
social conscience
social security
spare time
speculative investment
sport hunting
stable growth
straight dope
suicide doctor
sure bet
tax free
tax-loss benefits

temporary tax
think tank
too rich
understandable art
unequal partners
upscale strip joint
vacant lot
vaguely aware
vegetarian gourmet
Wall-Street wisdom

war ethics
weather forecast
windfall profits
wireless cable
wireless Internet
wishful thinking
working retirement
zero inflation
zero tolerance

ORDER FORM

A fabulous gift idea – even for yourself – because nothing beats a smile!

1001 Sidesplitting One-Liners & Some Wisdoms

Telephone orders: Call toll-free 1-800-84-LUCKY.
Please have your AMEX, Visa or MasterCard ready.
Online orders: www.dinesoneliners.com.
By mail: BCM, PO Box 636, Belvedere, CA 94920
(Please make checks payable to BCM Inc).

1 copy $19.95 each
2-5 copies $18.95 each
6-10 copies $17.95 each
11-20 copies $16.00 each
For larger orders please contact us directly for information.

For shipping and handling to the same address please add $3.95 for first-class delivery on single copies, $6.50 for 2-5 copies, $10.00 for 6-10 copies and $15.00 for 11-20 copies in the United States, Canada and Mexico. For overseas orders please add an additional $4.00 per book to above totals.

❑ Yes! Please rush me _____ copies of *"One Liners"* at
$_____ each, plus $_____ shipping for a total of $_____.

Name:_____

Address:_____

City_____ State/Prov_____ Zip Code_____

Country_____

Credit Card#:_____ Expiration _____

Signature:_____Check enclosed ❑

ORDER FORM

A fabulous gift idea – even for yourself – because nothing beats a smile!

1001 Sidesplitting One-Liners & Some Wisdoms

Telephone orders: Call toll-free 1-800-84-LUCKY.
Please have your AMEX, Visa or MasterCard ready.
Online orders: www.dinesoneliners.com.
By mail: BCM, PO Box 636, Belvedere, CA 94920
(Please make checks payable to BCM Inc).

> 1 copy $19.95 each
> 2-5 copies $18.95 each
> 6-10 copies $17.95 each
> 11-20 copies $16.00 each
> For larger orders please contact us directly for information.

For shipping and handling to the same address please add $3.95 for first class delivery on single copies, $6.50 for 2-5 copies, $10.00 for 6-10 copies and $15.00 for 11-20 copies in the United States, Canada and Mexico. For overseas orders please add an additional $4.00 per book to above totals.

❑ Yes! Please rush me _____ copies of *"One Liners"* at $_____ each, plus $_____ shipping for a total of $_____.

Name:_____

Address:_____

City_____ State/Prov_____ Zip Code_____

Country_____

Credit Card#:_____ Expiration _____

Signature:_____Check enclosed ❑

ORDER FORM

A fabulous gift idea – even for yourself – because nothing beats a smile!

1001 Sidesplitting One-Liners & Some Wisdoms

Telephone orders: Call toll-free 1-800-84-LUCKY.
Please have your AMEX, Visa or MasterCard ready.
Online orders: www.dinesoneliners.com.
By mail: BCM, PO Box 636, Belvedere, CA 94920
(Please make checks payable to BCM Inc).

> 1 copy $19.95 each
> 2-5 copies $18.95 each
> 6-10 copies $17.95 each
> 11-20 copies $16.00 each
> For larger orders please contact us directly for information.

For shipping and handling to the same address please add $3.95 for first-class delivery on single copies, $6.50 for 2-5 copies, $10.00 for 6-10 copies and $15.00 for 11-20 copies in the United States, Canada and Mexico. For overseas orders please add an additional $4.00 per book to above totals.

❏ Yes! Please rush me _____ copies of *"One Liners"* at $_____ each, plus $_____ shipping for a total of $_____.

Name:_____

Address:_____

City_____ State/Prov_____ Zip Code_____

Country_____

Credit Card#:_____ Expiration _____

Signature:_____Check enclosed ❏

ORDER FORM

A fabulous gift idea – even for yourself – because nothing beats a smile!
1001 Sidesplitting One-Liners & Some Wisdoms

Telephone orders: Call toll-free 1-800-84-LUCKY.
Please have your AMEX, Visa or MasterCard ready.
Online orders: www.dinesoneliners.com.
By mail: BCM, PO Box 636, Belvedere, CA 94920
(Please make checks payable to BCM Inc).

> 1 copy $19.95 each
> 2-5 copies $18.95 each
> 6-10 copies $17.95 each
> 11-20 copies $16.00 each
> For larger orders please contact us directly for information.

For shipping and handling to the same address please add $3.95 for first-class delivery on single copies, $6.50 for 2-5 copies, $10.00 for 6-10 copies and $15.00 for 11-20 copies in the United States, Canada and Mexico. For overseas orders please add an additional $4.00 per book to above totals.

❑ Yes! Please rush me ____ copies of *"One Liners"* at $_____ each, plus $_____ shipping for a total of $_____.

Name:_____

Address:_____

City_____ State/Prov_____ Zip Code_____

Country_____

Credit Card#:_____ Expiration _____

Signature:_____Check enclosed ❑